HULL : A DIVIDED CITY

Rugby League Matches between Hull Kingston Rovers and Hull Football Club 1899 — 1989

compiled by
Michael E. Ulyatt

Rugby League Statistical Records by
Bill Dalton

and
Foreword by Max Gold

HUTTON PRESS
1989

Published by the Hutton Press Ltd.
130 Canada Drive, Cherry Burton, Beverley
North Humberside HU17 7SB

Printed and bound by

Clifford Ward & Co. (Bridlington) Ltd.
55 West Street, Bridlington, East Yorkshire
YO15 3DZ

ISBN 0 907033 78 4

This book is dedicated to the memory of
Clive Sullivan, M.B.E.
the only player to score over 100 tries
and to receive a Challenge Cup Final Winner's
medal for both Hull and Hull Kingston Rovers
Rugby League Football Clubs

Rival Coaches, Roger Millward (Rovers) and Len Casey (Hull) on the right shake hands before the April 1987 Derby at the Boulevard. Photo by courtesy of Eddie Rolmanis.

CONTENTS

FOREWORD

No greater contrast exists than in the origins of Hull's two senior rugby league teams. Despite the contrast, the Club's records, particularly over recent years, have seemed to run on parallel courses and they have often contested important games, the most memorable of which was undoubtedly the 1980 Rugby League Challenge Cup Final held at Wembley, which not only left Hull a deserted city, but also gave rise to the idea behind this book.

Hull Football Club are one of the oldest rugby teams in the world —they are in fact a combination of the original Hull Football Club and an east Hull team called White Star. Hull Football Club were formed in 1865 by a group of ex-public school-boys and were closely connected with St. Mary's Church, Lowgate, Hull. Indeed the first teams put out included five of the sons of the then Reverend Scott of that church. Their first ground was at North Ferriby at the home of the Hutchinson family, and as one of the earliest players put it, "We would go anywhere and play under any rules for a game of football".

The game eventually became more organised. Hull Football Club were the first team in this area to join the Rugby Football Union. They played at many grounds, including one at Selby to ensure better West Riding fixtures and then, in 1881, having been beaten twice in the season by an east Hull team called White Star, it was resolved the Hull Football Club, should cease to exist. White Star, by joint agreement, took over the name Hull Football Club, and the old Hull Football Club members were eligible to join the new and growing organisation. White Star had been formed by a group of men mainly from more humble circumstances in 1873, who had quickly shown themselves to be skilled and fearless footballers, and their rise to local fame was such that they displaced Hull Football Club as the leading team, and took over its name, its players and its fixtures.

Hull Kingston Rovers, or as they were originally known, Kingston Amateurs, were formed by a group of shipyard apprentices and workers in 1882. The eldest was 18 years of age, and although records of the very early days are practically non-existent, their first few matches were probably played in Albert Street on the land now occupied by Ranks Mill, and the first ground of any importance was a football field at the back of the Star and Garter Pub, Hessle Road — where one touchline was the paving stones of the street. By 1892 they had a three year lease on the Boulevard and Hull Football Club (ex White Star) were playing in east Hull, though the localities were reversed in 1895.

Certainly in their early days Hull Kingston Rovers were the west Hull team and Hull Football Club the east Hull one.

By virtue of their greater seniority, Hull Football Club had a far superior playing list, including many of the major Yorkshire clubs such as Wakefield Trinity, Leeds St. John's, Batley, as well as teams from further afield such as Wigan, Clapham Rovers and Lansdowne of Ireland.

Rovers initially had to be content with fixtures against the lower teams of senior clubs — such local sides as Melbourne, Three Crowns, Cottingham, Beverley and Hessle — but their rise to fame can best be charted, particularly as a reputation as great cupfighters, by the history of the early fixtures concerning the two senior clubs.

Hull 'B'	v	Kingston Rovers 1st	1885/6	Rovers won
Hull 'A'	v	Kingston Rovers 1st	1886/7	Hull won
Hull 'A'	v	Kingston Rovers 1st	1887/8	Hull won
Hull 'A'	v	Kingston Rovers 1st	1888/9	Hull won
Hull 'A'	v	Kingston Rovers 1st	1888/9	Rovers won
Hull 'A'	v	Kingston Rovers 1st	1888/9	Draw
Hull 'B'	v	Kingston Rovers 'A'	1888/9	Rovers won
Hull 'B'	v	Kingston Rovers 'A'	1888/9	Rovers won
Hull 'A'	v	Kingston Rovers 1st	1889/90	Rovers won
Hull 'A'	v	Kingston Rovers 1st	1889/90	Hull won
Hull 'A'	v	Kingston Rovers 1st	1889/90	Hull won
Hull 'B'	v	Kingston Rovers 'A'	1889/90	Hull won
Hull 'B'	v	Kingston Rovers 'A'	1889/90	Draw
Hull 'B'	v	Kingston Rovers 'A'	1891/2	Rovers won
Hull 'A'	v	Kingston Rovers 1st	1893/4	Hull won
Hull 'B'	v	Kingston Rovers 'A'	1894/5	Rovers won
Hull 'B'	v	Kingston Rovers 'A'	1897/8	Rovers won

Hull won 7, Rovers 8 and 3 matches were drawn in matches played under Rugby Football Union rules before Hull joined the Northern Union League in 1895.

Most of these matches were either Hull and District Rugby Union or Hull Times cup ties.

Max Gold
Hull K.R. Director

ACKNOWLEDGEMENTS

It was Hull K.R. director Max Gold who first suggested I compile a book on the long and illustrious history of Hull F.C. and Hull Kingston Rovers derby Matches. That was in the summer of 1986 and since then I have been grateful for all the help and encouragement I have received from so many genuine rugby league supporters, especially from Bill Dalton with all his statistical work.
My thanks also go to Cyril Smith, Frank and Jean Morton, Colin Bielby, Len Young, Johnny Whiteley, John Moore, Ron Smalley, Ronnie Campbell, Len Casey, Ray Fletcher, John Helm, Jeff Schultz, and Colin Hutton for their 'Most memorable derby match' reminiscences.
Thanks to my wife Ann, for all her typing help, and to the Hull Local History Library.
Photographs by courtesy of the Hull Daily Mail, Eddie Rolmanis and Chris Park's collection.
Old Photographs copied by Malcolm Fussey of Hessle.

BIBLIOGRAPHY

Old Faithful. A History of Hull F.C. 1865-1987 .... Michael E. Ulyatt and Bill Dalton. Hutton Press 1988.
Hull Kingston Rovers Centenary History .... Michael E. Ulyatt. 1983.
Hull and Rovers through 88 seasons .... Christopher Elton. 1981.
Hull Daily Mail .... Various issues.
Yorkshire Post .... Various issues.
Rothman's Rugby League Yearbooks, 1981 to 1987 .... Raymond Fletcher and David Howes.

IN THE BEGINNING

Roman gladiatorial battles and Spanish bullfighting were put in the shade ninety years ago when Hull Kingston Rovers met Hull Football Club in their first ever Northern Union derby match, held at Rovers ground in Craven Street off Holderness Road on Saturday, 16th September 1899.

The City of Hull had never seen a sporting occasion like it. The match had been talked about for weeks beforehand. Hull F.C. had been founder members of the Northern Union in 1895 but Rovers had only been admitted into the Union for the 1899 campaign and rugby fans wondered whether the City could successfully support two teams. Indeed there had been talk of amalgamation in 1898. Vouchers had been issued for ground admission but the night before the match, enthusiastic supporters had slept in the best stand to ensure a good view of the match the next day; they were discovered on the Saturday morning and escorted out of the ground by police.

In Hull City centre, hansom cabs, rulleys and wagonettes gathered in Savile Street and at 12 noon the signal "Wagons roll" was given and the long procession got under way, over North Bridge and onto Holderness Road. Fares had doubled to 2d. for the journey and many supporters walked to save the money. Over 70 policemen lined the route to keep order and turned a blind eye to the over-crowding in the cabs and wagons. Gaily coloured cardboard shields were worn in supporters' hats exhorting the All Blacks (Hull F.C. then played in black shirts) or the Robins to "Play up".

At the ground itself, the gates were opened at 12.30p.m. and a band played from 1.30p.m. until 3.30p.m.

Considerate North Eastern railwaymen had left loaded wagons conveniently situated at the railway end of the ground to enable free viewing and these were soon packed with spectators.

A disappointing crowd, estimated to be in the region of 12,000 (which incidentally did not include any women, according to local newspaper reports) paying nearly £500 in receipts, saw referee Mr. Farrar of Halifax get the game under way. Hull F.C. were favourites for the match, having the heavier pack and the speedier backs. Surprisingly, only nine of the thirty players on view were local lads.

Wiles, Lemprière and Jacques of Hull and Kemp, Ripton, Tulloch, Ruddeforth, Fletcher and Stephenson of Rovers.

The narrow pitch at Craven Street did not suit Hull F.C. and Rovers strong tackling upset them. Tries from Starks and Kemp gave the Robins a 6-0 half-time lead and a drop goal from Tulloch in the second half, cancelled out by a Jacques goal for Hull F.C., gave Rovers an 8-2 victory in the first of many local derby matches.

Rovers also won the return match at the Boulevard and since then there have been 184 derby matches (excluding friendlies). Hull F.C. have won 91, Rovers 83 and 10 have been drawn.

The two clubs have met in 9 cup finals in various competitions over the years and these are chronicled in the following sections.

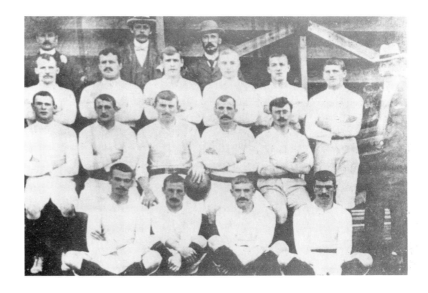

Hull Kingston Rovers N.U.F.C. 1899-1900. Picture shows the team which played in the first "local derby" versus Hull F.C. at Craven Street on Saturday 16th September 1899. Result Hull K.R. 8 points (1 goal, 2 tries) Hull F.C. 2 points (1 goal). Left to right, back row: Directors G. Gibbs, J. Mollekin, R.T. Hudson. Standing: J. Debney, Jack Rhodes, Anthony Starks, J. Stephenson, J. Noble, S. Ruddeforth, Director H. Mollekin. Seated: A. Windle, W. Guy, Albert Kemp (capt.) G. Fletcher, R.W. "Ginger" Jackson. In front: H. Sinclair, T. Ripton, H. Tulloch, J. Levett. Scorers: Hull K.R., Goal: Tullock (1), Tries: Starks (1), Kemp (1). Hull F.C., Goal: W. Jacques (1). Half-time score: Hull K.R. 6 points, Hull F.C. Nil.

Season 1901/02, Rovers versus Hull at Craven Street in the second round of the Challenge Cup. Hull won 10-5. Picture shows J.T. ("Fatty") Thompson (Hull half back) on the left challenging Jim Barry, Rovers' scrum half (with the ball), watched by (left to right) Anthony Starks, Jack Rhodes and Albert Kemp (all in white).

FIRST CUP FINAL MEETING

Rovers and Hull met in the final of the Yorkshire Cup in Season 1920/1, the first time both clubs had faced each other in a Northern Union final.

Rovers had reached the final by beating Bradford Northern (12-3), Leeds (8-2) and Dewsbury (8-5), while Hull received a bye in the first round and then beat Keighley (18-5) and Hunslet (31-5). The final was held at Headingley and fans left both Paragon and Cannon Street stations, decked out in red and white and black and white. Parties from Peel House Club, Tally Ho! Hotel, East Hull Working Men's Club, Kingston Bowling Club and the East Hull Conservative Club made the trip.

Both teams travelled on the same train, leaving Paragon Station at 11.47 am. with the Rovers' party in the front part of the train and Hull's towards the rear.

Rovers included 10 local players. A crowd of 20,000 paid £1,926. The match itself was a hard, dour affair with the muddy pitch favouring a forward battle. Full backs Osborne and Rogers were in outstanding form but with only minutes left and the score 0-0, Bradshaw coolly dropped a goal from fully 45 yards out and, in fading light, Rovers held out for a 2-0 victory. Arthur Moore received the cup, the first time a professional trophy in Northern Union had come to East Hull.

Both teams also travelled back together and attended a civic reception at Hull City Hall. It had been a great occasion for the City.

REVENGE FOR HULL F.C.

Hull and Rovers clashed again in the final of the Rugby League Championship in May 1921, again at Headingley. Rovers topped the League and thrashed Wigan 26-4 in the play-off semi-finals, and Hull beat Halifax 27-10 after finishing runners up in the League. Because of a restricted train service, only one excursion train, packed with 1,000 fans, left Paragon Station. Hull F.C. left the Imperial Hotel at 9.am by Charabanc and Rovers went by train at 8.30am., bound for the White Horse Restaurant in Leeds. Hull were bidding to retain the trophy. Rovers went ahead with a penalty goal from Gibson but Hull replied with tries from Bob Taylor, Stone and Devereaux while another goal from Gibson showed the half time score 9-4 to Hull.

Wyburn was injured but gallantly returned and he put Taylor in for his second try, goaled by Kennedy. Mulvey then scored under the posts for Rovers, goaled by Gibson, who added a penalty goal later to make the score 14-11. In a hard-fought last quarter, Kennedy landed a penalty goal but Rovers' Cook then went in for a try and with the score at 16-14, Gibson missed a kickable conversion. Although Rovers had finished strongly, Hull FC just about deserved their victory on the day, gaining ample revenge for their Yorkshire Cup defeat earlier in the season. Hull stopped off at the Lord Londesborough pub in Selby to celebrate and again at a pub in Market Weighton, returning to Hull about 11.pm where a large crowd was still waiting to welcome their heroes, and skipper Kennedy proudly held the trophy aloft. Some fans had spent five hours returning by train from Leeds.

There had been talk of holding the match at Hull City's Anlaby Road ground, but nothing seemed to come of it. Certainly the crowd of only 10,000 at Headingley would have been beaten!

Rovers' Steve Hartley makes a fine break in the 1981 Premiership Final at Headingley. The "Robins" won 11-7. Photo by courtesy of Hull Daily Mail.

FOUR MORE FINALS

A record crowd of 29,448 paid £47,529 at Headingley in May 1981 to see Rovers win the Premiership Trophy 11-7.

Hull had beaten Warrington and Castleford to reach the final while Rovers accounted for Widnes and St. Helens. It was the sixth all-Hull Final.

Phil Hogan opened the scoring with a try for Rovers in the 13th minute, goaled by Steve Hubbard before a sparkling 65 yard run and score by Steve Hartley gave Rovers an 8-0 lead. Woods kicked a penalty goal before Mike Smith broke through to score ten minutes after half-time. Charlie Stone drove well and his pass to Mick Crane enabled the ex-Rovers man to score a try which was goaled by Woods. Rovers held on to win in a frenzied last quarter and their skipper Len Casey won the Harry Sunderland 'man of the match' trophy.

The two clubs met in the final of the John Player Trophy in January 1982 when a crowd of 25,165 paid nearly £43,000 at Headingley. Hooker Ron Wileman scored the only try of the match with a blind-side break down the touchline and a run from halfway. Four goals from Lee Crooks and a drop goal from Tony Dean gave Hull a 12-4 victory. George Fairbairn kicked two penalties for Rovers. Hull's Trevor Skerrett was judged man of the match and Charlie Stone received the trophy after having been sent off earlier, together with Rovers' Roy Holdstock.

Season 1984/5 saw four derby matches. In the League, Rovers won 26-17 at Craven Park and 36-12 at the Boulevard. The teams also met in two cup finals. In October, Hull won the Yorkshire Cup for the third successive season. A crowd of 25,237 at Boothferry Park paid £68,639 to see a fluctuating match, Hull winning 29-12.

Rovers went into a 12-0 lead inside 30 minutes, with tries from Ian Robinson. George Fairbairn and David Hall. Hull then responded to Steve Norton's promptings and Lee Crooks touched down just before half time. Schofield had earlier kicked a penalty goal and he converted the try to leave the half time score:- Rovers 12 points, Hull 8 points. Shortly after the break, Gary Kemble sliced through the Robins' defence from half way to score a try, which was converted by Schofield, who also added a drop goal ten minutes later.

Further tries from Norton and Kemble with one goal from Schofield gave Hull a 25-12 lead before Steve Evans intercepted and raced 90 yards to score an unconverted try. Paul Rose was sent off after just coming on as a Hull sub. Peter Sterling was judged man of the match and a delighted Lee Crooks received the Yorkshire Cup. Rovers had their revenge in January when they won 12-0 to win the John Player Special Trophy for the first time.

A record crowd of 25,326 paid £69,555 at Boothferry Park to see Paul Harkin give a great display to win the man of the match award. Hogan, a late choice in the second row, scored a try in the first half and also touched down in the second half. Gary Prohm had scored a try in the 14th minute. Gavin Miller gave a typical Aussie performance, strong in defence and quick on attack. The match was played on a snow and ice surface. Rovers' skipper David Watkinson received the trophy.

Determination from Hull K.R.'s Phil Lowe in the 1981 Premiership Final at Headingley. Photo by courtesy of Hull Daily Mail.

Hull's Captain, Lee Crooks, scores a try in the 1984 Yorkshire Cup Final at Boothferry Park. Hull F.C. won 29-12, to win the trophy for the third successive season. Photo by courtesy of Hull Daily Mail.

Peter Sterling, "Man of the Match" in the 1984 Yorkshire Cup Final at Boothferry Park, looks for support from his Hull colleagues. Photo by courtesy of Hull Daily Mail.

George Fairbairn's first-half try for Rovers, despite Divorty's tackle, in the 1984 Yorkshire Cup Final at Boothferry Park. Photo by courtesy of Hull Daily Mail.

Phil Hogan scored two tries in Rovers' win in the 1985 John Player Trophy Final at Boothferry Park. Photo by courtesy of Hull Daily Mail.

REFLECTIONS ON THE ULTIMATE DERBY

A city had held its breath for seven days wondering if the first ever all-Hull Challenge Cup Final derby would take place at Wembley in May 1980.

Rovers had reached Wembley first, beating Halifax 20-7 in the first semi-final at Headingley. The following weekend Hull got there by beating cup favourites Widnes 10-5 at Swinton.

The unbelievable had happened: an all-Hull final at Wembley. What a run-up to the game. It seemed all the Rugby League media were in the City before the Final. Tickets for the game itself were like diamonds. It was the one topic of conversation in pubs and clubs throughout North Humberside and walking down Wembley Way on the day itself was akin to a Saturday down Whitefriargate; it seemed everyone knew one another. The banter was unceasing and the Metropolitan Police on duty marvelled that rival supporters dressed in black and white and red and white could link arms and stand and sit together in the Stadium. What an atmosphere! North London had never seen an afternoon like it: the fervour, the good humour, the determination to enjoy the day. The match itself was not a classic but it was always close and Rovers 10-5 victory brought joy to east Hull.

Both teams received a great welcome back to Hull the next day but the respective coaches, carrying players and officials, were as different as chalk and cheese. A dejected Sammy Lloyd reflected on the difficult goal kicks he missed which if successful would have brought the Airlie Birds success while Rovers' injured pair of skipper Roger Millward and Steve Hubbard raised the Cup on high. Rovers' fans have never allowed Hull F.C. supporters to forget the day but then the black and whites ask which team has won the most derby matches. The arguments and discussions will never end!

We've won the Cup! Hull K.R.'s Roy Holdstock lifts his captain, Roger Millward, in celebration after their Wembley win. Photo by courtesy of Hull Daily Mail.

Len Casey about to be tackled by Hull's Sammy Lloyd. Watching are David Watkinson and Alan Agar (right). Wembley 1980. Photo courtesy of Rugby Leaguer.

A TALE OF TWO CAPTAINS

Even though I have been involved in more than eighty local derby matches, one game still remains very vividly in my memory and that was one in which I was more of a villain than a hero.

The game was at Boothferry Park in 1955/6 season, when for financial reasons, Rovers had taken it there and forfeited home advantage. I was captain of Hull F.C. and we were clear favourites. It was a good season for us, as we finished fourth in the League, won the Championship play-off and reached the Final of the Yorkshire Cup while Rovers finished 24th in the League.

This derby match started off quite uneventfully, and towards the end of the first half the score was 4-4. Then, after an unsuccessful attempt at goal by Sam Evans, we re-started play from the twenty-five yard line with a drop-out. Tommy Finn tried to drop the ball in no-man's land behind the Rovers' line of defence but instead it dropped into the hands of prop forward Ken Grice and the next thing I knew was that Ken was running towards me with the ball. I

Colin Hutton, Hull F.C. player; later Coach and then Chairman of Hull K.R. Photo by courtesy of Hull Daily Mail.

was so confused with the train of events that I misjudged my attempted tackle on him and he promptly sidestepped me and scored alongside the posts. With all due respect to Ken (who I had the privilege of coaching later in my career at Craven Park) I think he would admit that the least of his qualities was a sidestep! Nevertheless, the try stood and Sam Evans converted it. Things were looking rather uncomfortable for us but by the middle of the second half we had taken command of the game and were leading 20-11.

The Rovers' centre, Bartliffe, scored a try, converted by Sam Evans and then came one of the more controversial incidents of the game. A scrum was formed five yards from the Hull line by referee Jackson of Barrow and the scrum collapsed. To all intents and purposes, the referee apparently signalled the scrum to be re-formed but as the players were picking themselves up from the floor, the Rovers' loose forward Jim Shires picked up the ball and promptly dived over the line, and to my (and everyone else's) amazement, the referee awarded a try. I remember one of the touch judges gleefully telling all and sundry the ball was going over from Sam Evans' conversion kick and Rovers led 21-20 with not long left to play.

Then came one of the most embarrassing moments of my career. Jim Tong, the Rovers' hooker and captain, infringed at a play the ball, and was penalised just outside of his own twenty-five yard line and directly in front of the posts. As I came to the attempted goal kick, Jim Tong said to me, "Well, it's either you or me, Colin," and as soon as I struck the ball for the goal kick I knew that it was me, because it sailed wide, outside of the right upright. Almost immediately the final whistle went and so ended the most embarrassing derby for me — I've certainly remembered it for a long time!

Colin Hutton,
Hull Kingston Rovers Chairman,
and former Hull F.C. player
and Hull Kingston Rovers coach.

BBC2 TV. FLOODLIT TROPHY

The last playing of the Final of the BBC2 TV Floodlit Trophy between Hull and Hull K.R. in 1979/80 is not a game I remember for its particular skills but rather for its 100% entertainment value.

Hull had reached the Final by beating Halifax 8-1 (preliminary round), Huddersfield 34-2, Leeds 16-9 and Leigh 9-6. Rovers got there with victories over Castleford 25-12, Keighley 41-15 and St. Helens 10-7.

A great final was in prospect with a capacity crowd of 18,500 (receipts £17,000) wondering whether Rovers could win the Trophy for the second time in three years, or if Hull could win it after three Semi-final defeats.

The Trophy was certain to come to the City of Hull and the game itself was a great advert for rugby league as it was televised nation-wide on a Tuesday evening.

Both teams put out strong sides including the late and great Clive Sullivan, Brian Lockwood, Keith Hepworth and 'Knocker' Norton. So the stage was set for a closely matched Final.

However, Hull FC took charge from the start and never let Rovers off the hook. The game was played at a cracking pace and to give credit to the Robins they never stopped trying and both teams gave the huge crowd their money's worth.

Rovers did get on the scoreboard with a try from Steve Hubbard but, although a runaway victory was never on, the Black and Whites never looked like losing and they won 13-3 after a try from Steve Dennison which I recall came after a run, kick through, pick-up from the bounce before he crashed over. We were not to know then of a scoreline to favour Rovers who won at Wembley not long afterwards, but that's another story!

I never really enjoy many derby games because although I have been a Hull FC fan for many years, I also watch Hull K.R. and do not like to see them lose!

Jeff Schultz

BEST PRE-WAR TEAMS

Len Young has been a Rovers' supporter since the early 1920's when the Robins' home ground was in Craven Street. He remembers season 1924/5 as his most memorable time. Rovers finished second in the League, reached the Challenge Cup Final and won the championship play-off. Len and his pals were on the popular side at Craven Park when Rovers thrashed Hull that season by a record 39-2, beating the previous highest win in season 1908/9 (35-4). He remembers willing Osbourne's kick over the bar to pass that score.

George Bateman, Hull K.R. right-wing three-quarter.

Len's best pre-war teams, together with reserve sides, are:-

Hull K.R.

1
L. Osborne
(G. Carmichael)

2
G. Austin
(G. Bateman)

3
J. Spamer
(J. Jordan)

4
J. Cook
(J. Hoult)

5
L. Harris
(Mick Eastwood)

6
H. Dale
(Mucker Clark)

7
J. McIntyre
(T. McGiever)

8
C.W. Westerdale
(L. Sharpe)

9
J. Ramsden
(F. Boagey)

10
B. Britton
(H. Binns)

11
G. Saddington
(F. Bielby)

12
F. Brindle
(H. Williams)

13
J. Feetham
(A. Moore)

*Joe Oliver,
Mr. "Old Faithful".
Photo by courtesy of
Hull Daily Mail.*

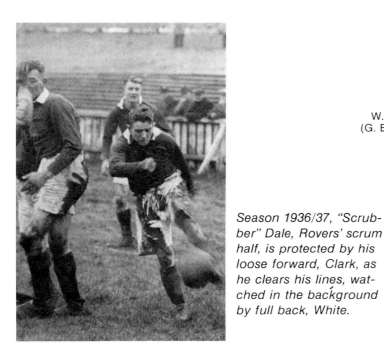

Season 1936/37, "Scrubber" Dale, Rovers' scrum half, is protected by his loose forward, Clark, as he clears his lines, watched in the background by full back, White.

Hull F.C.

1
F. Miller
(W. Teal)

2
W. Stone
(G. Bateman)

3
W. Batten
(J. Oliver)

4
R. Fifield
(J. Kennedy)

5
E. Gwynne
(J. Holdsworth)

6
E. Herberts
(E. Lawrence)

7
E. Caswell
(T. Johnson)

8
L. Thacker
(W. Stead)

9
G. Barlow
(S. Pickering)

10
H. Bowman
(T. Herridge)

11
E. Morgan
(C. Booth)

12
R. Taylor
(J. Dawson)

13
E. Ellerington
(A. Carmichael)

His choice of referee would be either Frank Renton or the Rev. W. Chambers.

19

Hull's Eddie Caswell, marked by three Rovers' players, passes the ball out towards his wing.

"GENTLEMAN JOHN'S" FIRST DERBY

Christmas Day 1950. What a day to play in your first derby match! Hessle Road and the fishing industry was vibrating again after the war and the whole of the dock area in East Hull was booming with trade.

For a local lad to move up from playing 'junior' rugby to taking part in a torrid local derby after just one professional match was a bit nerve-wracking to say the least.

Walking down to the Boulevard (note, walking — none of us had cars in those days) one caught the atmosphere a lot earlier than when one ran onto the pitch.

Half a dozen burly dockers walking behind me were making remarks like "you'll never be as good as Alec Dockar" (Rovers loose forward). Alec was a player I admired a great deal and we became firm friends. I reached the Boulevard that day an hour before kick-off and the atmosphere was already electric. I remember the antics of that stalwart Hull supporter 'Shep' and his entourage, pushing a black and white bedecked pram and getting all the Hull supporters singing 'Old Faithful'. Our coach Roy Francis in our pre-match team tactics talk didn't speak of merely 'a game' but more of 'a war' that was going to take place.

The game started with a crescendo of noise. What an atmosphere. The 'Threepenny Stand' was full and soon after the kick-off I was hit with a crash tackle by Ike Mills, Rovers' stand-off, and you could have lit all the lights on Hull's Paragon Station Christmas Tree with the electric shock that surged through me. I was fortunate to survive and the match finished at 3-3.

I played in, and coached, many more derby matches but I would have dearly loved to have played in the Wembley derby. The real credit goes to the supporters who have made the matches so special to play in. May they go on for evermore.

Johnny Whiteley,
former Hull FC Player and Coach
and Hull K.R. Coach.

CUP FINAL PRIDE

I suppose that from supporting the Airlie Birds as a boy to the end of my career with the Robins I must have watched or played in ninety to a hundred local derby games. The majority of those games have faded in my memory, but there are some I shall never forget. Out of those, my most memorable has to be the Yorkshire Cup Final of 1967.

During the mid-60's, Colin Hutton had blended together a side made up mainly of local players with a strategy based on fast wing-to-wing passing and backing-up the man in possession. This style of play had brought us thirteen consecutive victories leading up to the 1967 final, which included a win over the Australian Tourists. In the Cup we had beaten York, Dewsbury and Wakefield and having defeated Featherstone in the 1966 final we were determined not to relinquish our hold on the trophy.

The final which was played at Headingley on the 14th October 1967 in front of a near 17,000 crowd did not produce a feast of open rugby. It was, I remember, a cut-and-thrust affair with defences well on top. Our skipper Frank Foster, who had been out for a long time with an injured thumb, was declared fit for the game and was named as substitute. This meant that I continued to lead the side. I won the toss, and anticipating a bruising battle allowed Hull the benefit of a strong wind in the hope that it would give us the edge in the last quarter when legs began to tire.

It was clear that the Airlie Birds plan was to move up on us quickly and stop the ball reaching our fast backs — a task they achieved with marked success. A try to Chris Davidson in the first few minutes gave Hull the perfect start. Roger Millward brought the scores level with an interception try, and with penalty goals from John Maloney and Cyril Kellett the score was tied 5-5 at the interval. We brought on Frank Foster after the break which added more steel to our pack but we fell behind again when Davidson dropped a goal on the hour. Refusing to panic, we fought back and, after Dave Elliott and Colin Cooper had been stopped short of the line, we found the gap. Flash Flanagan got Terry Major away and he sent Alan Burwell over for the decisive try to give Rovers an 8-7 victory. So history had repeated itself with Hull K.R. winning by the narrowest margin, just as they did in the 1920 Yorkshire Cup Derby, which by coincidence was also played at Headingley.

I recall how proud I felt when presented with the Cup and afterwards at the reception at the Queen's Hotel, being required to give my first after-dinner speech — the "butterflies" started all over again.

John Moore. Former H.K.R. player and assistant coach.

John Moore and Bill Holliday with the Yorkshire Cup at Headingley. Photo by courtesy of Hull Daily Mail.

INTO OBSCURITY

My most memorable derby match? That's a tough one. I've seen so many great 'Ull'n Rovers battles that I could recall again and again. But if "most memorable" means the one that has lived longest in my memory then it must be a fairly obscure game about 40 years ago. The match is embossed on my mind for just one reason — a reserve team winger called Sanders scored all three tries for Hull in a 15-6 win at the Boulevard.

I remember little else about the game except that it was on a Good Friday, Tom Hart must have kicked the goals and Sanders caused a bit of a sensation with his hat-trick.

Sanders was soon returned to the A team and obscurity but he made a lasting impression on one skinny, little schoolboy. I have just checked the files and traced the match back to 1950 which means I was just nine at the time.

It is a measure of the impression Sanders' hat-trick made on me that on the other wing for Hull that day was Bruce Ryan — my first big sporting hero. I cannot remember Ryan doing anything in that match but, allowing for a schoolboy's greater imagination, the Australian remains the best threequarter I've seen play for Hull.

The match report of that 1950 game refers to it being a tough, uncompromising battle that the referee had some difficulty controlling. So what's changed?

Another early memory I have is that of Hull's players going on strike for more pay after beating Rovers but it was not until I looked up the 1950 match report that I realised I had forgotten it was the same game.

Although Hull finished above Rovers that season they still regarded beating the old enemy as extra special and asked for a bonus. Hull's board said "no", so the first team players went on strike with reserves filling the next two or three fixtures.

Raymond Fletcher
Yorkshire Post

MILLS WAS A JOLLY GOOD FELLOW

My most memorable "derby" match? You mean apart from a certain rewarding afternoon in North London in May 1980? One particular match stands out in special memory, and I'm sure it's not simply because it was one of the first "derby" games I ever witnessed.

It was Good Friday 1947 at Craven Park. Hull had already beaten Rovers twice that season and for some reason Rovers' selectors chose to reshuffle the back division to cover for the severe blow of being without full back and ace goalkicker, Wilf McWatt.

14,000 spectators in the ground, and it was estimated another 4,000 locked out, with further flavour added to the already boiling "derby" atmosphere by a small group of Hull fans bearing the corpse, of a Robin on top of a coffin, and rendering "The Death of Poor Cock Robin" on their penny whistles!

Joe Ramsden gave plenty of possession to Rovers, but they ran into a well drilled Hull defence. Centre Joe Sullivan, against run of play, carved a great opening for England wing-flyer, Albert Bowers. Then Jack Tindall forced his way over and Fred Miller easily goaled. For Rovers Billy Beaumont crossed in the corner, but when the sides turned round Jack Tindall went in again, and Miller's goal seemed to settle it at 13-3.

Rovers switched Maurice Daddy from centre (why was he playing there?) to his natural scrum half position. He shot straight through from a scrum, and the links were there to send Fred McBain racing over at the corner. But who would take the goal kick?

Utility back Ron Mills it was who positioned the ball only a few yards in from touch, and kicked a splendid goal. A couple of minutes later when Hull were penalised he landed another long-range kick.

13-10 and the atmosphere was electric. Rovers found another slight gap and McBain was in again, planting the ball down only inches from the flag to level the scores.

No one expected stand-in kicker Ron Mills to win the game by converting from the touchline, but judging the wind superbly he landed a wonderful goal.

I think it was former player Jack Spamer, still Rovers' record holder for most appearances in a career, who from the Well in front of the West Stand, led his fellow spectators in singing "For he's a jolly good fellow".

And just to prove what a jolly good fellow he was, when Hull erred again Ron Mills, again judging the wind to perfection, directed another kick from halfway straight over the red dot for his fourth goal

In those days a try was worth three points, and a goal however scored was worth two, and usually both qualified for nothing further than a congratulatory hand shake. None of the pat-a-cake palm-slapping displays, exhibitionist shimmy bottom-wiggling dancing or even fist-in-the-air salutes. But Ron Mills deserved his being chaired off at the end.

His achievement was all the more remarkable considering that in nine post-war seasons he only aggregated a further nine goals.

Frank Morton
(Hull K.R. programme editor)

A DRAMATIC 'LATE WIN' FOR ROVERS

My most memorable "local derby" takes me back to late in 1955, and a game at Boothferry Park. For several seasons Hull City had given Rovers a big boost financially by letting them have the use of Boothferry Park for their "home" game against Hull F.C. — and Rovers had lost them all.

For once this was a Saturday afternoon game, which was unusual for a "derby".

No-one could call Rovers a great team in those days. A bunch of local lads, of whom I was very proud, and a couple of bargain basement imports from the West Riding. Against them Hull had their much vaunted pack with Scott, Harris, the Drake twins, Markham and Whiteley, plus Colin Hutton at full back.

For half an hour the score hinged on goal kicks. It was 4-4 when Sam Evans missed a penalty just before halftime. Hull miskicked their drop out, which went straight to Rovers' prop Ken Grice who just ran straight through as the entire defence stood still. His try gave Evans an easy conversion.

9-4 to Rovers. But Hull came back, scoring three tries and taking the score up to 20-11. It looked as though we were in for another defeat at Boothferry Park!

Rovers retaliated with the best move of the day and centre Alan Bartliffe went over. Evans goaled. Four points in it and the minutes were ticking away. Still Rovers kept it up, and Hull hung on grimly. Parker's touch kick forced a scrum almost on Hull's line; everyone

was checking their watches which read 80 minutes; then second row man Jim Shires got possession and forced his way over. It now all hinged on the goal kick. Sam Evans took his time and booted a great goal from a wide angle.

21-20 to Rovers, but to everyone's amazement referee John Jackson from Barrow — never one of my favourite referees — insisted on play re-starting. Hull kicked deep, and Rovers were immediately penalised only yards in front of the posts. In those days the laws allowed the referee as sole timekeeper to extend time for time wasted, lost through accident or other cause.

I don't think Colin will want to be reminded of that incident, when he could hardly miss the easiest of goal kicks, but he did. We were delighted when he crossed over to the Eastern side of the City where he has given sterling service to Hull K.R.

Later we learned that Jim Shires, the scorer of the winning try, had played for over half the match with a broken bone in his wrist.

16,670 people attended that match and the teams were:

ROVERS: Buckle; Golder, Golding, Bartliffe, Garry; Thornton, Parker; Grice, Tong, Evans, Hall, Shires, Sutton.
HULL: Hutton; Bowman, Cooper, Riches, Watts; Moat, Finn; Scott, Harris, J. Drake, Markham, W. Drake, Whiteley.
Referee: J.W. Jackson of Barrow

Two very young Hull City Police cadets went with me on that day and I am very proud to think that they are now senior Police Officers and still very keen supporters of Hull K.R.

My proudest memory of all, I think, is when Hull K.R. went to Wembley in 1964. Many of the lads playing on that day had come up through Craven Park Juniors, and Frank and I were involved in the junior teams at Craven Park from their inception. I cried as the teams came out and was very proud to see players like Terry Major and Brian Tyson stepping out on to the Wembley pitch.

A lot of the camaraderie has now gone out of the "derby" matches. I loved being at the Boulevard in the late forties and early fifties when prior to the game, four men, dressed as undertakers, walked around the ground carrying a coffin with a 'dead Robin' on the top; and, of course, Roland walking around twirling his walking stick. Supporters of both sides packed together in the Threepenny Stand and were ribbing one another all the time — all for the fun of a "derby" game.

Jean Morton

Frank Morton and his wife Jean are keen Rugby League Supporters and have been members of many benefit committees for Hull Kingston Rovers players.

1960/61 season. Five of Hull F.C.'s "greats". Left to right: Jim Drake, Cyril Sykes, Tommy Harris, Bill Drake and Johnny Whiteley. Photo by courtesy of Hull Daily Mail.

the parade of the coffin, followed by strains of "The death of Cock Robin".

Scenes like this seemed to last only a short time and will never be repeated but the memories will never fade.

Cyril Smith,
a Hull F.C. supporter
since 1946.

MISSION IMPOSSIBLE

To search one's memory for the most memorable derby match would appear mission impossible after following one's team since the mid-forties. A priority would probably have to be a Hull victory but this would rule out my first derby final at Headingley in the Yorkshire Cup of 1967.

Victory for Hull would also rule out what was probably the City of Hull's finest hour when the derby match travelled to London for the Wembley Final. Everything was right on the day, good weather, a happy crowd of fans, but again the result spoilt Hull F.C.'s day.

Trying to find one's most memorable match would keep the fans talking in the pubs all night. What does an individual fan look for? Could it be the record gate for a First Division League match on April 17th 1981 when 18,500 saw the match at the Boulevard? Individual efforts tend to stick in your mind and certainly so when the try means victory for your side. Would it be the day when Hull's hooker, Ronnie Wileman, taking a play the ball on the best stand side at Headingley, jinked onto the blind side and scampered away down the touch line? It didn't seem possible that there was so far to go and no Rovers cover but none arrived in time and we had a victory for the Hull fans in the 1982 John Player Final.

A similar thing swung things in Hull's favour during the BBC2 Floodlit Trophy thanks to Steve Dennison. A break down the best stand side, a kick over the top, a favourable bounce, one man to beat and a try is scored, giving Hull victory on what turned out to be the last BBC2 Floodlit Trophy match in season 1979/80.

But probably the most lasting memories of the derby games have to be outside the game itself. In the very early days of going to see Hull F.C., with local derby matches every Christmas and Good Friday and travelling to the match, on approaching St. Matthews Church at the top of Boulevard, a large crowd was gathered with plenty of laughter and banter and in the middle of this crowd were two men dressed from top to toe in Hull F.C. colours. A sight like this I had never seen before and being nosey I hung around. Finally the crowd moved off and the two men carried off a coffin, draped in red and white, with a dead cock robin on top. The procession moved down to the ground and made a circuit of the pitch. An Airlie Bird was placed on the centre spot and reverence paid to the mascot. All this activity was helped along by the fans singing "Old Faithful" and

1ST ROUND OF THE RUGBY LEAGUE CUP — 4TH FEBRUARY, 1939 AT CRAVEN PARK.

As a supporter of Hull Kingston Rovers for many years, I have seen some wonderful and stirring local Derbys, but this was something special. Cup Tie fever had been building up for weeks and fans of both teams were speculating on the outcome.

The game was played before a crowd of almost 22,000 spectators, and the gate receipts were £1,349 which was a record amount for that time. It must rank as one of the best cup ties ever played and, I think, could be compared to the Wembley Cup Final of 1980.

One of Hull Football Club's all time greats, Joe Oliver, international centre of "give it to Joe" fame, at the end of an illustrious career transferred to Rovers and captained them in this memorable match.

The teams were:-

HULL F.C.	Miller; Hurley, Allen, Brogden, Bowers; Herbert, Johnson; Thacker, Barlow, Morrell, Booth, Dawson, Ellerington
RESERVES:	Wilson and Wray
HULL K.R.	White; Spamer, Oliver, McWatt, Milner; Eastwood, Morgan; Maskell, Ramsden, Blanchard, Clark, Beaumont, Cayser
RESERVE:	Bedford

Hull had a superb pack and were at peak form, so with Miller at full back and the former Leeds player Brogden at centre, were said to be odds-on favourites. Rovers for their part had played and won their last five home games.

Hull were the first to score. Dawson, the 15 stone forward, broke from his own line, kicked past full-back White and scored the first

*Shaking hands before the derby match in 1946/47,
(left to right) Harold Ellerington (Hull F.C. Captain),
Albert Harding (Broughton, Referee) and Joe Oliver
(Hull K.R. Captain).*

*1946/47 (left to right) Joe Rams-
den (Hull K.R.), Wilf Morrell (Hull
F.C.), Ray Maskill (Hull K.R.), Len
Clark (Hull K.R.), Harold Elle-
rington (Hull F.C.) with ball, Jack
Dawson (Hull F.C.) in back-
ground, and Jack Cayser (Hull
K.R.) making the tackle.*

try. This was quickly followed by one from Rovers, when Beaumont dived in for a try to level the score. Then Wilf McWatt put Rovers in front with a goal kick. Hull drew level, when Oliver was caught off-side and Fred Miller levelled the scores. Brogden almost beat the half-time whistle with a swift dash for the corner, but a desperate push into touch saved the day.

After the interval Hull threw even more power into the attack, but, though Johnson and Herbert repeatedly brought Brogden's speed into play, there was no way through.

Nobody proved a greater stumbling block to Hull's ambitions than the old hands, Oliver and Spamer. Oliver was playing his best match since joining Rovers, a sound pivot around which Rovers defence moved confidently. Oliver's faultless crosskicking to touch must have taken the heart out of his former colleagues.

Spamer kept a grip on Brogden and Bowers which nothing could break. Without taking away credit from the other members of the team, top marks must go to these two players.

Toward the end of the match, when a draw seemed certain, Miller made a bad clearance, the ball going to Milner who was held on the left wing; the ball travelled across the field — Morgan, Oliver and Eastwood handled brilliantly to provide Spamer with a narrow gap to score the all important try.

This was virtually the end of the match, which was played in the best spirit by both teams; neither trainer was ever on the field.

Final score: Rovers 8 Hull 5

Ron Smalley

COACHES EARN THEIR MONEY

It hasn't been my pleasure to witness too many derby matches on Humberside, but the few I have seen have all been full-blooded affairs.

I'll never forget, for example, going into the Hull FC dressing room in April 1985 both before and after the game and seeing the worried looks on the faces of Arthur Bunting and Kenny Foulkes.

"Fancy a game" said Arthur after running down the list of players who were actually turning out with injuries. I was out like a shot! "You're definitely in" he bellowed at me when I made a further check later to see who was going to be fit for the game against Castleford two days later.

It was a ridiculous period in which Hull had to play eleven games in April, including five in eight days, ten in sixteen days, and that really brought home to me how these fellows earn their money.

So do the coaches and that brings me to the derby game that lives most strongly in the memory.

It was at Craven Park in 1984, Good Friday I believe. The game was being televised and I had a roving commission on the touchline. Rovers had a fearsome pack including Broadhurst, Casey, Hogan and Hall. Behind them the multitudinous talents of George Fairbairn, Mike Smith, Gary Prohm and John Dorahy.

Hull turned up with Knocker Norton in a relatively inexperienced pack which included Lee Crooks and Gary Divorty.

Bunting's backs though were good enough to take any international arena: Kemble; Evans, Schofield, Leuluai, O'Hara; Topliss, Ah Kuoi.

Before the game both Arthur and Roger Millward had agreed that I could stick the microphone under their noses at any stage of the game.

Now that sounds fine in practice — but in reality — oh dear it can be very different.

I remember Kevin Ashcroft once offering a few words during a Warrington — Featherstone game, and even with the bleeper his comments about the referee still landed him in hot water!

There were some magnificent tries scored in this match — most of them by the Airlie Birds — so Arthur was only too happy to talk! Rovers got quite a pasting, 36-16 was the final score, so you can imagine every time I approached Roger it was in fear and trepidation, but he responded like the gentleman he is, paying tribute to some great players on the opposition, not making excuses, and generally making my job easy. It was a pleasure to witness a fine match and receive such warm response from two tremendous ambassadors for the clubs and the game as a whole.

by John Helm
(YTV Rugby League Commentator)

FANATICAL SUPPORTERS

Wembley 1980 was, to me, the greatest Derby of all. Not the actual game itself, but the build up, atmospherically. Unless you were born in Hull and had played professional rugby league for the twelve seasons prior to 1980 like I did, could you begin to imagine the electric tension and atmosphere before, through-out and after this particular Derby .... because it was a "first!" .... before 98,000 at the Wembley Stadium.

Over the years, I've always been proud to have worn the colours of both Hull Clubs. I know what it's like to win and lose in both strips. Every Derby was special to me, — red and white, or black and white. When you have won, you were number one; But, only until the next time. Hull's people will always talk rugby. They never let a Derby die. The constant craving for supremacy, or the chance for retaliation and vengeance, thrives in the most placid of supporters, (women reputedly being the most affected!). Not eating your breakfast on Derby Day because the bacon was red and white, or stamping across a zebra crossing to create the fallacy of 'pushing' the black and whites 'under' are just some of the strange behavioural antics some Hullensians are prone to. Fanatics!

Apart from the 1980 Wembley, the only other Derby game that really sticks in my mind is the winning of the Premiership against Hull at Headingley (my favourite ground). In the same game I won the Man-of-the-Match Award with so many good and highly respected players on both sides. On presentation, I was told I was judged for both ability and leadership, an honour I took reverently with the trophy.

I've played in the Bradford/Leeds Derby and coached a Wakefield Trinity/Leeds Derby; but nothing can compete with a Derby match between two halves of the same town, Hull F.C. and Hull K.R. Anyone who loves Rugby League loves a Derby.

Today's game is changing fast — and for the better, but surely I'm not on my own when I long for a little more blood and thunder these Derby Days!

Len Casey
former Hull FC and Hull KR
player and Hull FC coach.

Hull K.R. Captain, Len Casey, with the Slalom Lager Championship Trophy and the Premiership Trophy, won in season 1983/84. Hull finished runners-up in the League, one point behind the "Robins". Photo by courtesy of Hull Daily Mail.

And finally, as usual in Rugby League, the last word goes to the referee:-

MY MOST MEMORABLE DERBY MATCH

It is much easier said than done to choose your most memorable derby match. I went back to the first local derby I ever attended, Christmas Day 1945, when I remember Hull's Tommy Glynn scoring four tries, through to 1988 and after much mind searching I settled for the first all-Hull Yorkshire Cup Final for 47 years, played at Headingley, Leeds on 14th October 1967.

Rovers went into the match firm favourites, having beaten the Australian Touring side 27 points to 15 seven days before and were keen to retain the Cup they had won the previous year, but before the Robins had even touched the ball, Hull's Chris Davidson followed up at a play the ball and scored. The Airlie Birds were three points up in as many minutes.

Seven minutes later, Roger Millward levelled the scores when he intercepted and raced 40 yards. After penalties by John Maloney and Cyril Kellett, it was five points each at half time.

We then had to wait 20 minutes for this deadlock to be broken, until Chris Davidson dropped a goal, which counted two points at that time. The match became end to end rugby but both sides did not give an inch until the 74th minute when Rovers produced their best piece of football during the match; five players handled the ball before Alan Burwell went over to make the score 8-7 and after a further tense six minutes the Cup remained at Craven Park.

The match never reached a high standard of play but was a real nail biter with plenty of thrills for both sets of supporters. Since that day I have never attempted to forecast the result of a derby game!

An interesting point to the match was of the 27 players on the field during the game (Frank Foster was substitute for Rovers in the second half), nineteen were local born. They were, for Hull:- Oliver, Doyle-Davidson, Devonshire, Davidson, Harrison, McGlone, Edson, Macklin and Sykes; for Rovers:- Young, Moore, Elliott, Burwell, Cooper, Flanagan, Mennell, Lowe, Hickson and Major. The 'foreigners', for Hull:- Keegan, Maloney, Stocks and Brown, and for Rovers:- Kellett, Millward, Holliday and Foster.

Colin Bielby
A Hull Kingston Rovers supporter
since 1945

IN THE THICK OF IT

What a task, to try and choose a game from all of the Hull Derbies I was fortunate enough to control.

First of all I considered it an honour to referee either at the Boulevard or at Craven Park. When I was appointed to a Derby game I also regarded it as a sign that Rugby League had confidence in my ability to control a big game, for a Derby *is a Big Game*.

I always used to get there early to soak up the atmosphere. I used to walk out onto the pitch before the game loving the feeling of being in 'Rugby's Big Time', listening to the shouts of welcome from both sets of spectators:-

"Hey Campbell, Where's Your White Stick?"
"Get Back to Widnes, You Illegitimate Chap You!"

When I look back on my career I was lucky to be on the same field as some of 'the all time greats of Hull' and I have wonderful memories to treasure.

I was also proud to referee Benefit Matches at both grounds and I have also spoken at dinners at both clubs.

As far as I am concerned, all the Derbies were memorable and they all stand out, from the first, a Cup Tie when I sent three men off in 1978, to the last one in 1986 which, due to being postponed because of frost, was played on a 'bog' at Craven Park due to bad weather and six games in ten days.

I was involved in probably the most controversial incident in recent Derbies when I sent off Len Casey. He had become involved with the Touch Judge and was banned and missed the tour to Australia. Let me say now, I was deeply upset over that match because Len Casey was a player I admired; he gave no quarter and expected none. On the evidence of the Video, other players should have gone but I missed their part in the melee. The Touch Judge should not have approached Len; he should have kept well away. Players, when they have been sent off, are upset and are in a high state of tension. Len should have been allowed to cool down and things would have calmed down. Things were not helped by the presence of television, which allowed millions to see it, but to be fair, the presence of T.V. never bothered me, instead it used to put me on my toes.

When I was in the middle of a Hull Derby, I can honestly say I would not have changed places with anyone in the world. To me it was the *only* place to be. Amongst some of the best players in the World, in front of a packed Boulevard or Craven Park, roaring on their favourites, shouting abuse at me. Who cares? My skin used to crawl with the excitement.

In fact, just writing about it gives me that familiar thrill! God, I Wish I Was Still Out There.

Ron Campbell
(former Rugby League referee)

HULL v HULL KINGSTON ROVERS
A STATISTICAL HISTORY

The following pages contain the match details of every Hull v Rovers 'Derby', up to and including 2nd January 1989. For the sake of complete coverage, all matches are included: Friendly, Charity and Exhibition matches, as are those Wartime League fixtures during the 1914-18 Great War. These fixtures and the Players' appearances and scoring are *not* included in the index of Players' appearances and scoring. Nor do these matches count in the compilation of Match Records.

26th December 1899 — N.R.F.L.

HULL	0	v	ROVERS	3

W.H. Taylor	T. Smith
J. Driscoll	H. Tulloch *1 Try*
J. Tanner	S. Morfitt
W. Jacques	A.W. Robinson
R. Meek	T. Ward
J.T. Thompson	W. Guy
D. Frank	J. Levett
H. Wiles	A. Kemp
F. Cornish	A. Starks
R. Rhodes	J. Rhodes
W. Harmer	G. Fletcher
P. Fildes	J. Stephenson
G. Voyce	J. Debney
F. Gorman	E.W. Henson
C.A. Low	A. Windle

Halftime: 0-3   Ref: P. Farrar (Halifax)   Att: 20,000

16th September 1899 — N.R.F.L.

ROVERS	8	v	HULL	2

H. Sinclair	G. Sillis
S. Ruddeforth	C.C. Lempriere
H. Tulloch *1 Goal*	J. Driscoll
T. Ripton	J. Tanner
R.W. Jackson	W. Jacques *1 Goal*
W. Guy	D. Frank
J. Levett	J.T. Thompson
A. Kemp *1 Try*	F. Cornish
A. Starks *1 Try*	R. Parkinson
J. Rhodes	G. Voyce
G. Fletcher	R. Rhodes
J. Stephenson	F. Gorman
J. Noble	H. Wiles
J. Debney	W. Dale
A. Windle	P. Fildes

Halftime: 6-0   Ref: P. Farrar (Halifax)   Att: 14,000 (£500)

15th September 1900 — N.R.F.L.

ROVERS	11	v	HULL	20

T. Ward	W.H. Taylor
H. Tulloch *3 Goals*	J.Townend
C. Williams	J. Tanner
A.W. Robinson *1 Goal*	T. Dunn
R. Johnson	F.M. Crowe *1 Try*
W. Guy	J.T. Thompson *1 Try*
H. Kruger	D. Frank *2 Tries*
J. Rhodes	T. Stitt
A. Kemp	H. Woodhead
A. Starks	R. Parkinson *4 Goals*
J. Stephenson	P. Fildes
G. Fletcher *1 Try*	B. Hamm
J. Cole	F. Gorman
J. Debney	F. Spenceley
A. Windle	H. Wiles

Halftime: 5-10   Ref: W.W. McCutcheon (Oldham)   Att: 14,000

26th December 1900 — N.R.F.L.

HULL	11	v	ROVERS	2

W.H. Taylor	Johnson
J. Townend *3 Tries*	S. Morfitt
J. Driscoll	A.W. Robinson
J. Tanner	W. Phipps
J. Sharp	T. Ward
D. Frank	W. Guy
J.T. Thompson	J. Freeman
H. Woodhead	R. Rhodes
R. Parkinson *1 Goal*	A. Starks *1 Goal*
F. Spenceley	J. Stephenson
H. Wiles	A. Windle
F. Gorman	G. Fletcher
P. Fildes	J. Cole
T. Stitt	J. Debney
G. Voyce	G. Ellis

Halftime: 6-2   Ref: W.W. McCutcheon (Oldham)   Att: 23,000

23rd November 1901 — Friendly

HULL	5	v	ROVERS	0

W.H. Taylor	T. Smith
L. Parry	G.H. West
W. Jacques *1 Goal*	W. Madley
J. Driscoll	D. Murray
A. Hambrecht *1 Try*	R.W. Jackson
D. Frank	J. Barry
J.T. Thompson	C. Lewis
T. Stitt	A. Starks
R. Parkinson	A. Kemp
F. Miller	G. Fletcher
J. Wheeler	J. Stephenson
F.J. Bell	J. Gath
H. Fulton	W. Sims
J. Wade	A. Windle
F. Spenceley	J. Cornell

Halftime: 2-0   Ref: A. Brown (Brighouse)   Att: 12,000

11th October 1901 — Friendly

ROVERS	3	v	HULL	2

A. Townend	W.H. Taylor
G.H. West	A. Hambrecht
T. Smith	J. Driscoll
D. Murray	W. Jacques *1 Goal*
R.W. Jackson *1 Try*	J. Townend
J. Barry	D. Frank
W. Guy	J.T. Thompson
A. Starks	T. Stitt
J. Kemp	R. Parkinson
G. Fletcher	H. Fulton
J. Stephenson	J. Ritson
W. Sims	T. Bell
G. Ellis	F. Spenceley
J. Taylor	T. Wade
J. Gowan	P. Fildes

Halftime: 3-2   Ref: B. Ashton (Oldham)   Att: 9,000

22nd March 1902 — Northern Union Cup (2nd Round)

ROVERS	5	v	HULL	10

T. Smith *1 Goal*	W.H. Taylor
G.H. West	E.W. Brown
W. McConnell	A. Hambrecht
C. Lewis	W. Jacques *1 Goal*
W. Madley	L. Parry *2 Tries*
W. Guy	D. Frank
J. Barry *1 Try*	J.T. Thompson
A. Starks	T. Stitt
A. Kemp	P. Fildes
W. Stephenson	R. Parkinson *1 Goal*
J.W. Foster	H. Fulton
R. Rhodes	F. Spenceley
J. Taylor	F. Miller
W. Sims	J. Ritson
A. Windle	J. Wade

Halftime: 5-2   Ref: J. Bruckshaw (Stockport)   Att: 10,000

26th April 1902 — Friendly

HULL	14	v	ROVERS	6

W.H. Taylor	T. Smith *2 Goals*
S. Lewis *1 Try*	Wilson
E.W. Brown	C. Lewis *1 Goal*
W. Jacques *4 Goals*	W. Phipps
T. Bulless	W. Madley
D. Frank	J. Barry
J.T. Thompson	A. Shepherd
T. Stitt	A. Starks
A. Hambrecht *1 Try*	G. Fletcher
R. Parkinson	J. Stephenson
W. Harmer	J. Geenty
F. Spenceley	G. Ellis
R.W. Sanderson	W. Guy
L.G. Petrie	J. Small
H. Fulton	C.W. Asquith

Halftime: 7-0   Ref: H. Edmondson (Bradford)   Att: 4,000

17th January 1903 — N.R.F.L. (Division One)

ROVERS	10	v	HULL	0

H. Sinclair	W.H. Taylor
G.H. West *1 Try*	L. Parry
J. Gordon *1 Drop Goal*	W.J. Cook
S. Morfitt	R.T. Goddard
J.W. Read *1 Try*	R.W. Jackson
J. Barry	D. Frank
W.J. Carde	J.T. Thompson
A. Starks	J. Lewis
A. Kemp *1 Goal*	J. Wade
A. Windle	J. Ritson
J. Gath	F. Spenceley
G. Ellis	J. Harrison
J. Pickering	R. Rhodes
R. Townsley	H. Fulton
R. Goulding	C. Woodhead

Halftime: 8-0   Ref: P. Farrar (Halifax)   Att: 10,000

20th September 1902 — N.R.F.L. (Division One)

HULL	0	v	ROVERS	3

W.H. Taylor	G. Kirk
T. Bulless	G.H. West *1 Try*
W. Jacques	H. Sinclair
F.J. Cook	T. Smith
L. Parry	W. Phipps
G. Hall	W. Madley
R.T. Goddard	W. Guy
J. Lewis	J. Gath
R. Parkinson	G. Fletcher *(Sent off 60min)*
J. Wade *(Sent off 35min)*	W. Feetham
P. Fildes	R. Townsley
F. Miller	J. Cole
W. Langhorn	G. Ellis
W. Harmer	A. Starks
T. John	A. Kemp *(Sent off 35min)*

Halftime: 0-3   Ref: W. Robinson (Manningham)   Att: 14,000

19th December 1903 — N.R.F.L. (Division One)

ROVERS	2	v	HULL	3

H. Sinclair	W.H. Taylor
G.H. West	L. Parry *1 Try*
J. Gordon *1 Goal*	A. Moxon
W. Phipps	E.W. Brown
W. Madley	P. Carvill
J. Barry	J.T. Thompson
J.W. Read	F. Wood
G. Fletcher	J. Lewis
A. Kemp	J. Harrison
A. Windle	W.J. Langhorn
J. Pickering	H. Fulton *(sent off)*
R. Townsley	T. Carlisle
F. Gorman	R. Rhodes
G. Ellis	G.H. Lewis
R. Goulding	W. Hargreaves

Halftime: 2-0   Ref: W. Robinson (Manningham)   Att: 10,000

Jack Townend,
Hull F.C. Vice-Captain in 1898.

William Jacques, Hull F.C. and later
Hull K.R. trainer.

Ned Rogers, Hull F.C.

Frank Boylen (forward). Member of the
1910 tour team to Australia.

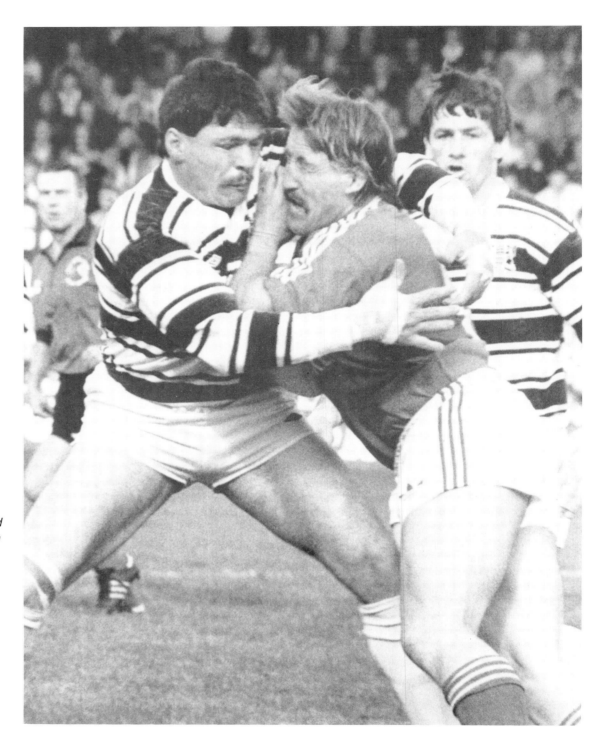

Crunch! Trevor Skerrett (Hull) and Mark Broadhurst (Rovers) meet in the tackle in the October 1983 Derby. Photo by courtesy of Eddie Rolmanis.

16th April 1904 — N.R.F.L. (Division One)

HULL	2	v	ROVERS	7

W.H. Taylor	H. Sinclair
R.W. Jackson	A. Carmichael *2 Goals*
E.W. Brown	W. Phipps
W. Bland	F. Marrow
P. Carvill	G.H. West
R.T. Goddard *1 Goal*	W. Guy *1 Try*
G. Hall	J. Gordon
J. Lewis	G. Fletcher
J. Harrison	A. Kemp
W.J. Langhorn	A. Starks
H. Fulton	J.W. Read
T. Carlisle	F. Gorman
R. Rhodes	G. Ellis
G.H. Lewis	A. Windle
F. Spenceley	R. Townsley

Halftime: 2-2   Ref: C. Gibson (Salford)   Att: large crowd
(Biggest of Season)

26th December 1904 — N.R.F.L. (Division One)

HULL	0	v	ROVERS	8

W.H. Taylor	A. Carmichael *1 Goal*
A.E. Freear	G.H. West
G. Hall	W. Phipps
W.J. Cook	A.W. Robinson
F. Goodfellow	W. Madley *1 Try*
J.W. Burchell	J. Barry
R.T. Goddard	J. Gordon
J. Ritson	A. Starks
J. Lewis	A. Kemp
G.H. Lewis	W.T. Osbourne
J. Major	D. Mullineaux *1 Try*
J. Harrison	A. Windle
G. Kilburn	A. Spackman
W.J. Langhorn	G. Ellis
W. Carroll	R. Townsley

Halftime: 0-8   Ref: J. Oakland (Barnsley)   Att: 15,000

10th December 1904 — Friendly

ROVERS	2	v	HULL	2

H. Sinclair	W.H. Taylor
G.H. West	F. Goodfellow *1 Goal*
J. Gordon	W.J. Cook
Bond	T. Jenkins
W. Madley	A.Freear
O. Chambers	J.W. Burchell
J. Barry *1 Drop Goal*	R.T. Goddard
A. Starks	J. Bilton
A. Kemp	W.J. Langhorn
W.T. Osbourne	J. Wade
D. Mullineaux	J. Hufton
A. Spackman	J. Harrison
A. Windle	G. Kilburn
R. Townsley	J. Lowe
G. Ellis	R. Rhodes

Halftime: 0-0   Ref: F. Renton (Hunslet)   Att: 4,000

21st April 1905 — N.R.F.L. (Division One)

ROVERS	6	v	HULL	11

H. Sinclair *1 Drop Goal*	W.H. Taylor
G.H. West	A.E. Freear *1 Try*
W. Phipps	W.J. Cook *1 Try*
A.W. Robinson	F. Goodfellow *1 Goal*
W. Madley *2 Goals*	T. Jenkins
J. Barry	J.W. Burchell
J. Gordon	G. Hall
A. Kemp	J. Ritson *1 Try*
A. Windle	J. Lewis
W.T. Osbourne	J. Harrison
A. Spackman	G. Kilburn
G. Ellis	J. Hufton
F. Gorman	W.J. Langhorn
R. Townsley	H. Fulton
D. Mullineaux	J. Major

Halftime: 6-0   Ref: J. Crompton (Bradford)   Att: 10,000

26th December 1905 — N.R.F.L.

HULL	4	v	ROVERS	5

W.H. Taylor	H. Sinclair
G. Hall	G.H. West *1 Goal*
F. Goodfellow *2 Goals*	W. Phipps *1 Try*
W. Hall	W. Madley
W.J. Cook	W.F. Jowett
J. Brunyard	J. Gordon
J.W. Burchell	O. Chambers
J. Harrison	A. Starks
W. Carroll	A. Windle
J. Hufton	J. Gath
H. Fulton	W. Bent
G. Kilburn	C.J. Hambrecht
J. Lewis	D. Mullineaux
J. Major	H. Sherwood
W. Hargreaves	W.T. Osbourne

Halftime: 4-5   Ref: W.W. McCutcheon (Oldham)   Att: 12,000

13th April 1906 — N.R.F.L.

ROVERS	4	v	HULL	17

H. Sinclair	W.H. Taylor
G.H. West	L. Parry
W. Phipps	W.J. Cook
D. Rees	W. Hall
W. Madley	A.E. Freear
J. Barry	J.W. Burchell *1 Try*
J. Gordon	R.T. Goddard *4 Goals*
A. Starks *2 Goals*	J. Harrison
J. Gath	W. Carroll
C.J. Hambrecht	H. Fulton
W. Bent	G. Kilburn
H. Sherwood	J. Major
D. Mullineaux	R. Rhodes
A. Windle	W. Hargreaves
A. Spackman	P. Carvill *2 Tries*

Halftime: 2-2   Ref: W.W. McCutcheon (Oldham)   Att: 12,000

8th February 1906 — Friendly
(in aid of Local Unemployment Fund)

HULL	0	v	ROVERS	5

W.H. Taylor	W. Madley
P. Carvill	W. Phipps
W.H. Pullen	D. Rees
L. Parry	W.F. Jowett
J.W. Burchell	J. Barry *1 Goal*
T.W. Goddard	J. Gordon
W.J. Cook	A. Lofthouse
W. Hall	H. Ansell *1 Try*
T. Jenkins	A. Starks
J. Lewis	G. Ellis
W. Carroll	D. Mullineaux
H. Carroll	W. Bent
Sutton	W.T. Osbourne
Bailes	A. Spackman
J.Major	J. Dawson

Halftime: 0-0   Ref: J. Oakland (Wakefield)   Att: 3,500

26th December 1906 — N.R.F.L.

HULL	8	v	ROVERS	0

W.H. Taylor	A. Carmichael
L. Parry	G.H. West
W.J. Cook	W. Phipps
A. Harrison *1 Try*	D. Rees
E. Rogers *1 Try; 1 Goal*	G. Pratt
H. Wallace	A. Lofthouse
W. Burchell	J. Barry
S.J. Banks	A. Spackman
W.T. Osbourne	N.H. Smith
J. Major	H. Sherwood
P. Carvill	S. Sherwood
W. Carroll	J. Gath
G. Kilburn	A. Windle

Halftime: 0-0   Ref: W.W. McCutcheon (Oldham)   Att: 10,000

29th March 1907 — N.R.F.L.

ROVERS	21	v	HULL	10

A. Carmichael	*3 Goals*	E. Rogers	*2 Goals*
G.H. West		T. Bell	*1 Try*
J. Barry		G. Hall	
S. Read	*1 Try*	W.J. Cook	
W.H. Dilcock	*2 Tries*	T. Jenkins	
J. Fenton		H. Wallace	
A. Lofthouse		C.W. Larkins	
J. Gath		W.T. Osbourne	
A. Starks	*1 Try*	C.W. Eggett	
C.J. Hambrecht		G. Kilburn	
J. Hotham		P. Carvill	*1 Try*
S. Sherwood		W. Carroll	
G. Pratt	*1 Try*	R.A. Parkes	

Halftime: 13-3   Ref: R. Robinson (Bradford)   Att: 9,000

26th December 1907 — N.R.F.L.

ROVERS	0	v	HULL	7

A. Carmichael		W.H. Taylor	
G.H. West		W. Holder	
W. Phipps		G. Cottrell	
W.J. Read		T. Bruce	*2 Goals*
G. Pratt		E. Rogers	
A. Booth		H. Wallace	
R.W. Cavill		W. Anderson	
J. Gath		W. Carroll	
T.E. Richardson		T. Herridge	
W. Biggs		J. Owen	*1 Try*
G. Ellis		J. Major	
Tom.Taylor		G. Kilburn	
A. Windle		H. Fulton	

Halftime: 0-0   Ref: J.H. Smith (Widnes)   Att: 11,000

12th October 1907 — N.R.F.L.

HULL	8	v	ROVERS	6

W.H. Taylor		A. Carmichael	
J.W. Castles		G. Pratt	*1 Try*
G. Cottrell		W. Phipps	*1 Try*
T. Bruce	*1 Goal*	D. Rees	
E. Rogers	*2 Tries*	W.F. Jowett	
H. Wallace		A. Booth	
W.F. Anderson		J. Barry	
W. Holder		A. Starks	
T. Herridge		J. Gath	
J. Owen		A. Spackman	
G. Kilburn		J. Hotham	*(sent off)*
H. Fulton		A. Windle	
W. Carroll		G. Ellis	

Halftime: 0-3   Ref: E. Tonge (Swinton)   Att: 14,000

26th December 1908 — N.R.F.L.

HULL	33	v	ROVERS	7

W.H. Taylor		A. Carmichael	*2 Goals*
J. Dechan	*2 Tries*	C. Brain	*1 Try*
G. Cottrell		F. Barron	
E. Rogers	*3 Tries; 2 Goals*	J.W. Read	
G. Rogers	*1 Try*	J. Sedgwick	
H. Wallace	*1 Goal*	R.W. Cavill	
W. Anderson		A. Booth	
T. Herridge	*1 Try*	A. Spackman	
W. Holder		W. Biggs	
F. Boylen	*1 Try*	G. Unsworth	
H. Walton	*1 Try*	T. Taylor	
H. Fulton		G. Ellis	
J. Major		R.H. Barlow	

Halftime: 11-7   Ref: J.H. Smith (Widnes)   Att: 16,000 (£395)

9th April 1909 — N.R.F.L.

ROVERS	35	v	HULL	4

A. Carmichael *6 Goals*	R.S. Brown
P. White	E. Atkinson
R. Hughes *1 Goal*	J. Devereux
P. Thomas *2 Tries*	T. Bruce *2 Goals*
F. Barron *2 Tries*	A. Morton
J. Barry	J. Jones
A. Lofthouse	C.W. Larkins
W. Sandham *2 Tries*	M. Appleyard
C. Brain	G. Purcheon
A. Spackman	J. Owen
G. Pratt	W. Carroll
A. Moore *1 Try*	H. Fulton
G. Unsworth	J. Major

Halftime: 13-2   Ref: B. Ennion (Wigan)   Att: 15,000 (£350)

27th December 1909 — N.R.F.L.

ROVERS	15	v	HULL	12

A. Carmichael *3 Goals*	W.H. Taylor
W.H. Dilcock	A. Morton
R.W. Dakin	J. Devereux
P. Thomas	G. Rogers
F. Barron *1 Try*	E. Rogers *1 Try; 3 Goals*
R. Hughes	H. Wallace *1 Try*
R. Sykes	W. Anderson
C. Brain *1 Try*	T. Herridge
A. Mann	F. Boylen
A. Moore	G. Connell
A. Spackman *1 Try*	H. Fulton
W. Sandham	R. (Dick) Taylor
C.J. Hambrecht	W.T. Osbourne

Halftime: 13-5   Ref: J.H. Smith (Widnes)   Att: 16,000 (£370)

9th October 1909 — N.R.F.L.

HULL	16	v	ROVERS	5

W.H. Taylor	A. Carmichael *1 Goal*
A. Morton *1 Try*	F. Barron
J. Devereux *1 Try*	P. Thomas
G. Rogers	R. Hughes
E. Rogers *2 Tries; 2 Goals*	J.W. Read
H. Wallace	J. Gordon
W. Anderson	A. Booth
T. Herridge	A. Mann
F. Boylen	A. Spackman
G. Connell	W. Sandham
H. Fulton	C.J. Hambrecht
G. Stevenson	A. Moore *1 Try*
R. (Dick) Taylor	W. Huskins

Halftime: 13-2   Ref: J.H. Smith (Widnes)   Att: 14,000

1st October 1910 — N.R.F.L.

HULL	8	v	ROVERS	8

E. Clarkson	A. Carmichael *1 Goal*
G. Cottrell	W.H. Dilcock *1 Try*
G. Connell	R. Hughes
A. Morton	P. Thomas
E. Rogers *1 Goal*	W. Hyam *1 Try*
A. Francis *1 Try*	T. Surman
H. Wallace	T.E. Richardson
W. Holder	A. Mann
R. (Dick) Taylor	A. Spackman
D. Galloway	J. Blackmore
T. Herridge	W. Huskins
H. Walton *1 Try*	W. Sandham
F. Boylen	C. Brain

Halftime: 3-3   Ref: B. Ennion (Wigan)   Att: 14,000 (£438)

26th December 1910 — N.R.F.L.

ROVERS	5	v	HULL	5

A. Carmichael *1 Goal*	E. Clarkson
W.H. Dilcock *1 Try*	E. Sykes
P. Thomas	T. Dinsdale
R. Hughes	J. Devereux
W. Hyam	E. Rogers *1 Goal*
R. Jones	F. Battersby
B. Craven	H. Wallace
J. Blackmore	G. Connell
W. Huskins	W. Holder
A. Mann	T. Herridge
A. Spackman	S. Britton
C. McDonald	F. Boylen *1 Try*
A. Moore	R. (Dick) Taylor

Halftime 5-5   Ref: B. Ennion (Wigan)   Att: 11,000 (£380)

7th October 1911 — N.R.F.L.

HULL	4	v	ROVERS	19

E. Clarkson	A. Carmichael *4 Goals*
A. Francis	G. Spivey *1 Try*
J. Devereux	R. Hughes *1 Try*
G. Rogers	W. Hyam
E. Rogers *2 Goals*	C. Brain *1 Drop Goal*
H. Wallace	T. Surman *1 Try*
F. Hughes	B. Craven
G. Connell	A. Moore
T. Herridge	A. Mann
A. Allen	W. Sandham
R. (Dick) Taylor	W. Huskins
H. Fulton	J. Blackmore
W. Holder	A. Spackman

Halftime: 4-5   Ref: W.W. McCutcheon (Oldham)   Rec: £408

22nd April 1911 — Friendly

ROVERS	37	v	HULL	8

A. Carmichael *8 Goals*	G. Connell
G. Spivey *1 Try*	A. Francis
R. Hughes	J. Devereux
P. Thomas *2 Tries*	G. Cottrell
C. Brain	E. Rogers *1 Try; 1 Goal*
B. Craven	F. Hughes
T. Surman	F. Battersby
A. Mann	T. Herridge
A. Moore *1 Try*	W. Holder
W. Sandham *1 Try*	F. Boylen *1 Try*
W. Huskins *1 Try*	D. Galloway
A. Spackman *1 Try*	R. (Dick) Taylor
J. Blackmore	S. Britton

Halftime: 12-8   Ref: E.H. Smirk (Wigan)   Att: 11,000 (£234)

26th December 1911 — N.R.F.L.

ROVERS	18	v	HULL	5

A. Carmichael *3 Goals*	E. Clarkson
G. Spivey *1 Try*	E.J. Schofield
R. Hughes	E. Rogers *1 Goal*
W. Hyam *1 Try*	C.H. Cappleman
C. Brain	G. Cottrell
A. Watson	A. Barrow *1 Try*
B. Craven *1 Try*	G. Rogers
W. Sandham	G. Connell
A. Mann *1 Try*	A. Allen
A. Moore	S. Britton
W. Huskins	F. Boylen
J. Blackmore	A. Grice
P. Boltman	W. Holder

Halftime: 12-0   Ref: E. Robinson (Bradford)   Att: 13,000

Ivor Watts, Hull F.C. Photo by courtesy of Hull Daily Mail.

Alan Burwell, Hull K.R.

*"Flash" Flanagan.
Photo by courtesy of
Hull Daily Mail.*

*Jim Drake.
Photo by courtesy of
Hull Daily Mail.*

John Maloney of Hull F.C.
Photo by courtesy of Hull Daily Mail.

28th September 1912 — N.R.F.L.

ROVERS	18	v	HULL	0

A. Carmichael *2 Goals*	E. Rogers
W.H. Dilcock	J. Harrison
R.G. Hicks	G. Cottrell
R. Hughes	H. Gilbert
C. Brain	S. Darmody
R. Sykes	W. Higgins
I.L. Dean *1 Goal*	W. Anderson
A. Moore	T. Herridge
A. Mann	A.J. Merry
L.C. Trump	A. Grice
W. Huskins *1 Try*	F. Boylen
D. Lewis *1 Try*	R. (Dick) Taylor
W. Sandham *1 Try*	G. Connell

Halftime: 5-0   Ref: J.F. May (St. Helens)   Att: 15,000

4th October 1913 — N.R.F.L.

HULL	5	v	ROVERS	2

E. Rogers *1 Goal*	A. Carmichael *1 Goal*
J. Devereux	R.G. Hicks
W. Batten	W. Shiel
H. Gilbert	P. Thomas
A. Francis	H. Lord
G. Rogers	C.L. Gillie
W. Anderson	I.L. Dean
R. (Dick) Taylor	A. Mann
W. Holder	A. Moore
T. Herridge	W. Huskins
A. Grice *1 Try*	W. Sandham
J. Hammill	C. Brain
S. Darmody	L.C. Trump

Halftime: 5-0   Ref: G.F. Dickenson (Halifax)   Att: 23,000 (£658)

26th December 1912 — N.R.F.L.

HULL	7	v	ROVERS	5

E. Rogers *2 Goals*	A. Carmichael *1 Goal*
A. Francis	W.H. Dilcock
H. Gilbert	R. Hughes
G. Cottrell	R.G. Hicks
J. Harrison	C. Brain
W. Higgins	I.L. Dean
W. Anderson	R. Sykes
T. Herridge	A. Mann
A. Allen	A. Moore *1 Try*
A. Grice	W. Sandham
W. Holder	W. Huskins
R. (Dick) Taylor	D. Lewis
S. Darmody *1 Try*	L.C. Trump

Halftime: 5-5   Ref: F. Renton (Hunslet)   Att: 16,000
(£478.8.11)

26th December 1913 — N.R.F.L.

ROVERS	9	v	HULL	5

A. Carmichael *3 Goals*	E. Rogers *1 Goal*
E. Hodgson *1 Try*	G. Cottrell
R.G. Hicks	W. Batten
F.W. Oliver	H. Gilbert
H. Lord	A. Francis *1 Try*
T. McGiever	G. Rogers
A. Watson	W. Anderson
W. Horner	R. (Dick) Taylor
A. Moore	W. Holder
W. Sandham	J.P. Oldham
C. McDonald	T. Herridge
L.C. Trump	A. Grice
C. Brain *(sent off)*	S. Darmody *(sent off)*

Halftime: 2-0   Ref: J.W. Whiteley (Wakefield)   Att: 12,000 (£320)

26th September 1914 — N.R.F.L.

HULL	16	v	ROVERS	7

E. Rogers *2 Goals*	F.W. Oliver
H. Gilbert *1 Try*	W. Bradshaw
S. Deane	J.H. Prescott
W. Batten *1 Try*	D. Vaughan
J. Harrison *1 Try*	H. Lord
T. Milner	I.L. Dean *1 Goal*
W. Anderson	T. McGiever
T. Herridge	A. Mann
W. Holder	W. Huskins
R. (Dick) Taylor	L.C. Trump
J. Hammill	W.T. Wootton *1 Goal*
J.E. Wyburn *1 Try*	J. Lowe
S. Darmody	C. McDonald *1 Try*

Halftime: 3-2   Ref: A. Hestford (Broughton R.)   Att: 15,000 (£439)

26th December 1914 — N.R.F.L.

ROVERS	8	v	HULL	14

A. Carmichael	E. Rogers *1 Goal*
L. Fussey	A. Francis
D. Vaughan *2 Tries*	H. Gilbert *1 Try*
J. Gilmore	W. Batten
H. Lord	J. Harrison *2 Tries*
I.L. Dean	T. Milner
T. McGiever	W. Anderson
A. Mann	T. Herridge
W. Huskins	W. Holder
W.T. Wootton *1 Goal*	F.L. Perrett
L.C. Trump	J. Hammill
T.H. Brown	J.P. Oldham *1 Try*
J. Lowe	J. Beasty

Halftime: 0-11   Ref: A. Hestford (Broughton R.)   Att: 10,000 (£241)

31st October 1914 — Yorkshire Cup (2nd Round)

HULL	11	v	ROVERS	5

E. Rogers *1 Goal*	A. Carmichael *1 Goal*
A. Francis *1 Try*	L. Fussey
J. Devereux *1 Try*	D. Vaughan *1 Try*
S. Darmody	F.W. Oliver
J. Harrison *1 Try*	H. Lord
T. Milner	J.H. Prescott
W. Anderson	I.L. Dean
T. Herridge	A. Mann
W. Holder	W. Huskins
R. (Dick) Taylor	W.T. Wootton
J. Hammill	L.C. Trump
J.E. Wyburn	L. Lowe
J.P. Oldham	C. McDonald

Halftime: 3-5   Ref: R. Jones (Widnes)   Att: 14,000 (£432.12.6)

2nd October 1915 — War League

ROVERS	8	v	HULL	13

F.W. Oliver	E. Rogers *2 Goals*
L. Fussey *1 Try*	J. Harrison *1 Try*
T.H. Brown	W. Batten
J. Gilmore *1 Try*	S. Deane
W. Bradshaw *1 Goal*	A. Francis *2 Tries*
A. Watson	T. Milner
W. Clark	G. Rogers
A. Mann	T. Herridge
W. Huskins	W. Holder
L.C. Trump	J.P. Oldham
A. Spackman	J.E. Wyburn
C. McDonald	J. Beasty
A. Palframan	H. Havelock

Halftime: 3-5   Ref: W.K. Hirst (Dewsbury)   Att: 10,000

25th December 1915 — War League

HULL	27	v	ROVERS	5

E. Rogers *1 Goal*	F.W. Oliver
A. Francis	L. Fussey *1 Try*
W. Batten *1 Try*	W. Bradshaw
J. Devereux	J. Gilmore
J. Harrison *1 Try*	H. Lord
T. Milner	R.W. Cavill
S. Deane	T. McGiever
T. Herridge *2 Tries*	W. Huskins
J.P. Oldham	W. Clark
J.E. Wyburn *1 Try*	L.C. Trump
F. Boylen	A. Palframan *1 Goal*
J.E. Kennedy *2 Tries; 2 Goals*	T.H. Brown
J. Beasty	C. McDonald

Halftime: 10-0   Ref: W.K. Hirst (Dewsbury)   Att: 10,000

21st April 1916 — War League

HULL	14	v	ROVERS	8

E. Rogers	F.W. Oliver
A. Francis *2 Tries*	L. Fussey
W. Batten	W. Bradshaw *1 Goal*
T. Bruce	J. Gilmore *2 Tries*
J.E. Kennedy *1 Try; 1 Goal*	H. Lord
T. Milner	T. McGiever
G. Rogers	Parker
T. Herridge *1 Try*	L.C. Trump
W. Holder	J. Lowe
J.P. Oldham	W. Clark
J.E. Wyburn	Dannatt
F. Boylen	Evans
J. Beasty	T.H. Brown

Halftime: 5-3   Ref: R. Robinson (Bradford)   Att: 9,000

15th January 1916 — War League

ROVERS	2	v	HULL	13

F.W. Oliver	E. Rogers
L. Fussey	A. Francis
W. Bradshaw *1 Goal*	W. Batten
J. Gilmore	T. Bruce *1 Try*
H. Lord	W. Stringer *1 Try*
T. McGiever	T. Milner
W. Clark	S. Deane
A. Mann	T. Herridge
W. Huskins	W. Holder
T.H. Brown	F. Boylen *1 Try*
A. Palframan	J. Beasty
W. Kennedy	J.E. Wyburn
Barnes	J.E. Kennedy *2 Goals*

Halftime: 0-5   Ref: F. Renton (Hunslet)   Att: 8,000

23rd September 1916 — War League

HULL	29	v	ROVERS	6

E. Rogers	Holt
A. Francis *1 Try*	L. Fussey
W. Batten *1 Try*	R.G. Hicks
J. Devereux *1 Try*	Exley
J. Holdsworth	Swift
G. Rogers *1 Try*	R.W. Cavill
T. Milner	Hulme *1 Try*
T. Herridge	A. Mann
W. Holder *1 Try*	W. Clark
F. Boylen	Dannatt
J. Beasty	W. Kennedy
J.E. Kennedy *1 Try; 4 Goals*	A. Moore *1 Try*
J.P. Oldham *1 Try*	Taylor

Halftime: 18-3   Ref: A. Brown (Wakefield)   Att: 6,000

28th October 1916 — War League

ROVERS	15	v	HULL	5

F.W. Oliver	T. Bruce
Harrison	A. Francis
W. Bradshaw *1 Try; 3 Goals*	J. Devereux
J. Gilmore *1 Try*	G. Rogers
H. Lord	J. Holdsworth
T. McGiever	T. Milner
J.H. Prescott	Rushton
A. Palframan	T. Herridge
W. Clark *1 Try*	W. Holder
Taylor	F. Boylen
F. Bielby	J.E. Kennedy *1 Goal*
W. Kennedy	J. Beasty *1 Try*
Holt	J.E. Wyburn

Halftime: 3-5   Ref: A. Brown (Wakefield)   Att: 5,000

6th April 1917 — War League

HULL	20	v	ROVERS	5

L. Evans	F.W. Oliver
A. Francis	Harrison
J.E. Kennedy *4 Goals*	W. Bradshaw *1 Try; 1 Goal*
J. Devereux *1 Try*	J. Gilson
J. Holdsworth *1 Try*	Swift
Rushton	Hulme
G. Rogers *1 Try*	Newman
W. Holder	L.C. Trump
J.E. Wyburn	W. Clark
W. Kennedy	Heathcote
McFarlane	Lilley
H. Garrett	Holt
F. Boylen *1 Try*	Taylor

Halftime: 13-5   Ref: W.K. Hirst (Dewsbury)   Att: 5,000

25th December 1916 — War League

ROVERS	6	v	HULL	3

Evans	Chapman
Harrison	Martin
W. Bradshaw *1 Try*	E. Rogers
F. Barron	A. Francis
Swift	J.E. Kennedy
F.W. Oliver *1 Try*	T. Milner
Hume	J.P. Oldham
A. Palframan	J. Beasty
W. Clark	W. Holder
Dannatt	J.E. Wyburn
Heathcote	H. Garrett *1 Try*
F. Bielby	F. Boylen
Holt	W. Kennedy

Halftime: 3-0   Ref: F. Renton (Hunslet)   Att: 4,000
The game was abandoned after 63 minutes owing to a late kick-off and gathering darkness.

9th April 1917 — War League

ROVERS	12	v	HULL	5

F.W. Oliver	L. Evans *(Bradford)*
Bratley	Winstanley *(Swinton)*
W. Bradshaw *3 Goals*	G. Rogers *1 Goal*
Hulme	A. Francis
Swift	J. Holdsworth
Newman *1 Try*	Talbot *(Swinton) 1 Try*
Kilgarris	Rushton
Holt	F. Boylen
F. Bielby	Barrett
Heathcote *1 Try*	Bolton
Lilley	Price
Gibbins	Rowley
Taylor	Blewer *(Swinton)*

Halftime: 7-5   Ref: A. Brown (Wakefield)   Att: 5,000

15th September 1917 — War League

ROVERS	8	v	HULL	19

Jackson	L. Evans
W. Bradshaw *1 Try; 1 Goal*	Meheux *1 Try*
Boyd	G. Rogers *1 Try*
A. Watson	G. Cottrell
Swift	J. Holdsworth
Hulme	Gomersall *1 Try*
Empson *1 Try*	Newbould
Taylor	W. Holder *1 Try; 1 Goal*
F. Bielby	F. Boylen
Holt	J.E. Wyburn
Wilson	H. Garrett *1 Try*
C. McDonald	W. Kennedy *1 Goal*

Halftime: 5-11   Ref: T. Johnson (Bramley)   Att: 4,000

8th December 1917 — War League

ROVERS	10	v	HULL	22

W. Forrester	Meheux
J. Cook *1 Try*	J. Holdsworth
Harrison	W. Batten *2 Tries*
F. Bielby	J. Devereux *1 Try*
Allen	A. Francis *2 Tries*
Kershaw *1 Try*	T. Milner
Mulchinook	Newbould
C. McDonald	W. Holder
F. Boylen	J.E. Kennedy *2 Goals*
Smith *1 Goal*	Martin *(Keighley)*
Newsome *1 Goal*	W. Kennedy *1 Try*
Bloomer *(York)*	Lilley

Halftime: 10-8   Ref: W.K. Hirst (Dewsbury)   Att: 1,500

3rd November 1917 — War League

HULL	33	v	ROVERS	2

Greenwood	W. Forrester
A. Francis *3 Tries*	Land
J. Devereux	W. Bradshaw *1 Goal*
W. Batten *1 Try*	J. Cook
J. Holdsworth *5 Tries*	Bird
T. Milner	Richardson
Newbould	Thompson
W. Holder	C. McDonald
J.E. Kennedy *3 Goals*	Wilson
F. Boylen	Bloomer *(York)*
W. Kennedy	Holt
J. Beasty	F. Bielby

Halftime: 16-0   Ref: J. Wilson (HKR)   Att: 2,000

25th December 1917 — War League

HULL	14	v	ROVERS	6

Chapman	J. Cook
A. Francis *1 Try*	L. Fussey
W. Batten *2 Tries*	W. Bradshaw
T. Bruce	T. Bateman
J. Holdsworth	Goodfellow
Newbould *1 Try*	R.W. Cavill
T. Dinsdale	Mulchinock
W. Holder	F. Bielby *1 Try*
J.E. Kennedy *1 Goal*	Smith
W. Kennedy	F. Boylen *1 Try*
J. Beasty	G. Pratt
Martin *(Keighley)*	Blower

Halftime: 8-6   Ref: F. Renton (Hunslet)   Att: 2,000

B. Chalkley (Rovers full back) kicks for goal, watched by Referee George Phillips, at Booth-ferry Park in April 1953. Hull won 11-2. Photo by courtesy of Hull Daily Mail.

October 1959. A combined Hull and Rovers side lost 29-9 to the Australian tourists at Boothferry Park. Back row (left to right): Moat, Garton, Bateson, Harris. Centre: Elliott, Holland, Sykes, Scott, Jenkin. Front: Wilson, Matthews, Paul, Drake. Photo by courtesy of Hull Daily Mail.

Two men who did so much for Rugby League in Hull. Rovers' Chairman, Wilf Spaven (right) and Hull F.C.'s Chairman, Ernest Hardaker, May 1960. Photo by courtesy of Hull Daily Mail.

November 1960. Members of Hull K.R., Hull F.C. and Hull City who lost 7-6 to a team of Yorkshire County cricketers at Craven park. The soccer match was in aid of the benefit funds for Yorkshire's Brian Close and Rovers' Ken Grice. Back row (left to right): Jim Drake, Cyril Sykes, Bob Coverdale, Billy Bly, Dennis Durham, Sam Evans. Front row: Tommy Harris, Graham Paul, Ken Grice, Colin Hutton, Wilf Hassall. Photo by courtesy of Hull Daily Mail.

9th February 1918 — War League

ROVERS	11	v	HULL	20

Holt	Griffin
J. Cook	A. Francis *1 Try*
W. Bradshaw *1 Goal*	Harris *2 Tries*
Swift	Meheux
Harrison *1 Try*	J. Holdsworth *2 Tries*
Mulchinock	A. Barrow
Kershaw *1 Try*	Newbould *1 Goal*
F. Bielby *1 Try*	W. Holder
Bloomer *(York)*	J.E. Wyburn
F. Boylen	W. Kennedy *(sent off)*
G. Pratt	Lilley
I.L. Dean	Martin *(Keighley) 1 Try*

Halftime: 11-3   Ref: A. Brown (Wakefield)   Att: 2,000

29th March 1918 — War League

HULL	6	v	ROVERS	5

Holt *(HKR)*	W. Bradshaw *1 Goal*
Pendle	Harrison
Dinsdale *(Bramley)*	Hughes *(Bramley)*
W. Batten	Marshall *(Leeds)*
J. Holdsworth	J. Lyman *(Dewsbury)*
J. Hulme	Ward *(Bramley)*
Richardson *(HKR) 1 Try*	Muscroft *(Bramley)*
W. Holder	C. McDonald
J. Kennedy	F. Boylen
Lilley *(HKR)*	Bloomer *(York)*
Martin *(Keighley)*	F. Bielby *1 Try*
Giblin *(HKR) 1 Try*	G. Pratt

Halftime: 0-5   Ref: F. Renton (Hunslet)   Att: 5,000

25th December 1918 — Friendly

HULL	21	v	ROVERS	5

J. Holdsworth	Holt
A. Francis *1 Try*	W. Bradshaw *1 Goal*
J.E. Kennedy *3 Goals*	L. Fussey *1 Try*
W. Batten *2 Tries*	Beal
E. Watson	G. Spivey
T. Milner	R. Hughes
J. Hulme	A. Cork
A. Grice	J. Blackmore
J. Beasty *1 Try*	W.T. Wootton
J.P. Oldham *1 Try*	G. Pratt
J. Gresswell *(Batley)*	F. Boylen
W. Kennedy	Bloomer *(York)*

Halftime: Ref: C.W. Eastman (Hull)   Att: 2,000

26th December 1918 — Friendly

ROVERS	2	v	HULL	29

A. Carmichael	J. Holdsworth
L. Fussey	J.E. Kennedy *2 Tries; 3 Goals*
F. Barron	J. Devereux
Beal	W. Batten *2 Tries*
W. Bradshaw *1 Goal*	A. Francis *1 Try*
A. Cork	T. Milner
R. Hughes	J. Hulme
J. Blackmore	W. Holder
W.T. Wootton	A. Grice *2 Tries*
G. Pratt	J. Beasty
F. Boylen	J.P. Oldham
Bloomer *(York)*	J.R. Gresswell *(Batley) 1 Goal*

Halftime: 2-13   Ref: C.W. Eastman (Hull)   Att: 5,000

18th April 1919 — N.R.F.L. (Yorkshire Section)

HULL	11	v	ROVERS	7

J. Forrester	G. Austin
A. Francis *1 Try*	Peak
J.E. Kennedy *1 Try; 1 Goal*	L. Fussey
W. Batten	A. Watson
J. Holdsworth	W. Bradshaw *1 Try; 1 Goal*
T. Milner	R. Sykes
J. Hulme	J.H. Prescott
W. Kennedy	A. Mann
J.P. Oldham	W.T. Wootton *1 Goal*
J. Beasty *(sent off)*	W. Clark
T. Herridge	A. Gibson
J.E. Wyburn	F. Boylen
H. Garrett *1 Try*	F. Bielby

Halftime: 6-4   Ref: B. Ennion (Wigan)   Att: 16,000 (£735)

19th July 1919 — Friendly (Peace Day Celebration)

HULL	13	v	ROVERS	5

J. Holdsworth	G. Austin
A. Francis	Murray
J.E. Kennedy *1 Try; 2 Goals*	C.W. Westerdale
W. Batten *1 Try*	A. Watson
E.T. Nolan *1 Try*	L. Fussey
J.A. Holliday	J.H. Prescott
J. Hulme	T. Bateman *1 Try*
W. Holder	A. Palframan *1 Goal*
J.E. Wyburn	F. Bielby
H. Garrett	W. Clark
J.P. Oldham	Ackrill
R. Elvin	A. Moore
S. Tinkler	T.H. Brown

Halftime: 8-0   Ref: W. Eastman (Hull)   Att: 5,000

21st April 1919 — N.R.F.L. (Yorkshire Section)

ROVERS	5	v	HULL	24

G. Austin	E.T. Nolan
Peak	A. Francis *1 Try*
L. Fussey	J.E. Kennedy *1 Try; 3 Goals*
A. Watson *(sent off)*	W. Batten *2 Tries*
W. Bradshaw	J. Holdsworth
J.H. Prescott	T. Milner *2 Tries*
W. Allen	J. Hulme
A. Mann	W. Holder
F. Boylen	J. Beasty
W.T. Wootton *1 Goal*	J.E. Wyburn
A. Gibson	W. Kennedy
W. Clark *1 Try*	A. Grice
F. Bielby	H. Garrett

Halftime: 0-13   Ref: F. Renton (Hunslet)   Att: 11,000 (£428.14.8)

27th September 1919 — N.R.F.L.

HULL	8	v	ROVERS	8

J. Holdsworth	G. Austin
A. Francis *1 Try*	W. Bradshaw *1 Goal*
W. Batten	F. Bielby
J. Kennedy *1 Goal*	A. Watson
E.T. Nolan *1 Try*	L. Fussey
J.A. Holliday	T. McGiever *1 Try*
T. Milner	T. Bateman
T. Herridge	A. Moore
F. Newsome	W. Huskins
W. Holder	W. Sandham
J.P. Oldham	W.T. Wootton *1 Try*
J.E. Wyburn	F. Boylen
H. Garrett	A. Gibson

Halftime: 8-8   Ref: C. Peel (Bradford)   Att: 18,000   Rec: £1,065 (Record)

25th December 1919 — N.R.F.L.

ROVERS	5	v	HULL	16

G. Austin	E. Rogers	*1 Goal*
W. Bradshaw *1 Goal*	A. Francis	*1 Try*
F. Bielby	J.E. Kennedy	*2 Tries; 1 Goal*
R. Keegan	W. Batten	
J. Cook	J. Holdsworth	*1 Try*
T. McGiever	E. Caswell	
H. Kitson	T. Milner	
R. Boagey	T. Herridge	
W. Clark	J.P. Oldham	
H. Bullock	J.E. Wyburn	
F. Boylen	A. Grice	
A. Gibson	J. Beasty	
A. Moore *1 Try*	H. Garrett	

Halftime: 0-11   Ref: C. Peel (Bradford)   Att: 14,000 (£800)

2nd October 1920 — N.R.F.L.

ROVERS	6	v	HULL	15

G. Austin	E. Rogers	
H. Mulvey	G. Todd	
J. Cook	J.W. Markham	
D. Cooper	J.E. Kennedy	*1 Try; 3 Goals*
W. Bradshaw *1 Try*	J. Holdsworth	*1 Try*
T. McGiever *(sent off)*	J. Humphries	
W. Clark	E. Caswell	
A. Moore *(sent off)*	J. Beasty	
R. Boagey	H. Hewson	
C.W. Westerdale	H. Taylor	
J.R. Wilkinson	J.E. Wyburn	
F. Bielby *1 Try*	R. (Bob) Taylor	
A. Gibson	H. Garrett	*1 Try*

Halftime: 0-9   Ref: Mr. Mills (Oldham)   Att: 14,000

8th May 1920 — Friendly (Great War Trust Fund Shield)

HULL	18	v	ROVERS	10

J. Holdsworth	G. Austin	*1 Try*
A. Francis *2 Tries*	A.E. Wilkinson	
J.E. Kennedy *1 Try; 3 Goals*	L. Harris	
W. Batten	J. Cook	
J.W. Markham	W. Bradshaw	*2 Goals*
J. Hulme	W. Clark	
T. Milner	Spicer	
T. Herridge	R. Boagey	
E.C. Shield	*A.N. Other*	
W. Holder	A. Moore	*1 Try*
F. Newsome	H. Wilkinson	
J.E. Wyburn	J.R. Wilkinson	
H. Garrett *1 Try*	F. Boylen	

Halftime: 11-5   Ref: C. Peel (Bradford)   Att: 10,000 (£500)

27th November 1920 — YORKSHIRE CUP FINAL
(at Headingley, Leeds)

HULL	0	v	ROVERS	2

E. ROGERS	L. OSBORNE	
A. FRANCIS	L. HARRIS	
W.H. STONE	G. AUSTIN	
W. BATTEN	J. COOK	
J. HOLDSWORTH	W. BRADSHAW	*1 DROP GOAL*
E. CASWELL	T. McGIEVER	
T. MILNER	W. CLARK	
J. BEASTY	J.H. WILKINSON	
H. HEWSON	R. BOAGEY	
H. TAYLOR	J.R. WILKINSON	
R. (Bob) TAYLOR	F. BIELBY	
J.E. WYBURN	A. MOORE	
J.E. KENNEDY	A. GIBSON	

Halftime: 0-0   Ref: A. Hestford (Broughton)   Att: 20,000 (£1,936)

25th December 1920 — N.R.F.L.

HULL   **4**   v   **ROVERS**   **8**

E. Rogers	L. Osborne
J.E. Kennedy *2 Goals*	L. Harris
W.H. Stone	G. Austin *2 Tries*
W. Batten	J. Cook
J. Holdsworth	H. Mulvey
T. Milner	T. McGiever
E. Caswell	W. Clark
T. Herridge	J.H. Wilkinson
F. Newsome	R. Boagey
R. (Bob) Taylor	J.R. Wilkinson
J.E. Wyburn	A. Moore
A. Grice	A. Gibson *1 Goal*
H. Garrett	F. Bielby

Halftime: 0-5   Ref: A. Brown (Wakefield)   Att: 25,000 (£1,706)

12th May 1921 — Friendly (War Charity)

HULL/ROVERS   **'LOCAL' PLAYERS: 13**   v   **HULL/ROVERS**   **'IMPORTED' PLAYERS: 10**

E. Rogers *(Hull)*	W. Bradshaw *(Rovers)*
L. Harris *(Rovers)*	H. Mulvey *(Rovers)*
J. Cook *(Rovers)*	E. Caswell *(Hull)*
J.E. Kennedy *(Hull) 1 Try; 2 Goals*	J. Devereux *(Hull, Captain)*
G. Austin *(Rovers)*	W.H. Stone *(Hull) 2 Tries*
T. McGiever *(Rovers)*	J. Humphries *(Hull)*
W. Clark *(Rovers) 1 Try*	T. Milner *(Hull)*
J. Beasty *(Hull) 1 Try*	R. Shields *(Hull)*
F. Westerdale *(Rovers)*	J. Ellis *(Hull)*
F. Bielby *(Rovers)*	A. Grice(Hull)
H. Garrett *(Hull)*	F. Newsome *(Hull)*
J.H. Wilkinson *(Rovers)*	R. Boagey *(Rovers)*
A. Moore *(Rovers, Captain)*	R. (Bob) Taylor *(Hull) 1 Try*

Halftime: 5-10   Ref: F. Renton (Hunslet)   Att: 6,000

7th May 1921 — R.L. CHAMPIONSHIP FINAL
(at Headingley, Leeds)

HULL   **16**   v   **ROVERS**   **14**

E. ROGERS	L. OSBORNE
J. DEVEREUX *1 TRY*	L. HARRIS
J.E. KENNEDY *2 GOALS*	G. AUSTIN
W. BATTEN	J. COOK *1 TRY*
W.H. STONE *1 TRY*	H. MULVEY *1 TRY*
E. CASWELL	T. McGIEVER
T. MILNER	W. CLARK
J. BEASTY	J.H. WILKINSON
J.A. ELLIS	F. BIELBY
F. NEWSOME	R. BOAGEY
R. (Bob) TAYLOR *2 TRIES*	A. MOORE
J.E. WYBURN	A. GIBSON *4 GOALS*
H. GARRETT	J.R. WILKINSON

Halftime: 9-4   Ref: A. Brown (Wakefield)   Att: 10,000 (£1,320)

1st October 1921 — N.R.F.L.

HULL   **3**   v   **ROVERS**   **13**

E. Rogers	L. Osborne
J. Holdsworth	L. Harris *1 Try*
T.E. Gwynne	G. Austin
J.E. Kennedy	J. Cook
G. Todd *1 Try*	W. Bradshaw *2 Goals*
E. Caswell	T. McGiever
T. Milner	W. Clark
J.E. Wyburn	J.R. Wilkinson
J. Ellis	C.W. Westerdale *1 Try*
J. Beasty	A. Gibson
F. Newsome	J.H. Wilkinson
R. (Bob) Taylor *(sent off)*	F. Bielby *(sent off)*
H. Garrett	A. Moore *1 Try*

Halftime: Not known   Ref: T. Johnson (Bramley)   Att: 20,000

26th December 1921 — N.R.F.L.

ROVERS	0	v	HULL	18

L. Osborne	E. Rogers
L. Harris	J. Holdsworth *1 Try*
G. Austin	J.E. Kennedy *1 Try; 3 Goals*
J. Cook	W. Batten
H. Mulvey *(sent off)*	W.H. Stone
J. McGlone	E. Caswell *1 Try*
W. Clark	T. Milner
J.R. Wilkinson	G. Oliver
A. Gibson	J. Ellis
F. Boagey	J. Beasty
C.W. Westerdale	R. (Bob) Taylor *1 Try*
F. Bielby	E. Morgan
A. Moore	J.E. Wyburn

Halftime: 0-18   Ref: T. Johnson (Bramley)   Att: 11,000

7th October 1922 — N.R.F.L. (at Craven Park, Hull)

ROVERS	7	v	HULL	10

L. Osborne *2 Goals*	E. Rogers
L. Harris	J. Holdsworth *1 Try*
R. Rees	J.E. Kennedy *2 Goals*
J. Cook	W. Batten
G. Austin	W.H. Stone
J. Hoult	T.E. Gwynne
J. McIntyre	E. Caswell *1 Try*
J.H. Wilkinson	H. Bowman
C.W. Westerdale	G. Oliver
F. Boagey	G. Howlett
G. Van Rooyen	E. Morgan
W. Clark	J. Beasty
F. Bielby *1 Try*	H. Garrett

Halftime 0-5   Ref: F. Renton (Hunslet)   Att: 22,282 (£1,300)

11th March 1922 — R.L. Cup (2nd Round)

ROVERS	0	v	HULL	10

L. Osborne	E. Rogers
L. Harris	J. Holdsworth
G. Austin	J.E. Kennedy *1 Try; 2 Goals*
R. Rees	W. Batten
J. Cook	W.H. Stone
T. McGiever	E. Caswell
W. Clark	T.E. Gwynne
J.R. Wilkinson	J. Beasty
A. Gibson	J. Ellis
J.H. Wilkinson	G. Oliver
C.W. Westerdale	E. Morgan
F. Bielby	R. (Bob) Taylor *1 Try*
A. Moore	H. Garrett

Halftime: 0-0   Ref: A. Hestford (Broughton)   Att: 18,000 (£1,000)

21st October 1922 — Yorkshire Cup (1st Round)

ROVERS	14	v	HULL	2

L. Osborne *4 Goals*	E. Rogers
L. Harris *1 Try*	W.H. Stone
R. Rees *1 Try*	J.E. Kennedy *1 Goal*
J. Cook	W. Batten
G. Austin	J. Holdsworth
J. Hoult	T. Milner
T. McGiever	E. Caswell
J.H. Wilkinson	G. Oliver
C.W. Westerdale	H. Bowman
J.R. Wilkinson	J. Beasty
F. Boagey	E. Morgan
F. Bielby	R. (Bob) Taylor
A. Moore	H. Garrett

Halftime: 9-2   Ref: B. Ennion (Wigan)   Att: 21,000 (£1,160)

*Eva Hardaker Charity Cup match, August 1963 at Craven Park.
John Taylor, Rovers, held by Terry Devonshire with Hull's Clive
Sullivan and Rovers' Graham Paul on the left and Hull's Jim
Macklin on the right. Hull won 15-11. Photo by courtesy of Hull
Daily Mail.*

Rovers' Brian Tyson well-tackled by Hull's Arthur Keegan at the Boulevard. Photo by courtesy of Hull Daily Mail.

25th December 1922 — N.R.F.L.

HULL	19	v	ROVERS	6

F. Samuel	L. Osborne
W.H. Stone *1 Try*	L. Harris
J.E. Kennedy *2 Goals*	R. Rees
W. Batten	J. Cook
J. Holdsworth	G. Austin
S. Whitty	J. Hoult *1 Try*
E. Caswell *2 Tries*	J. McIntyre *1 Try*
H. Bowman	J.H. Wilkinson
E. Morgan *2 Tries*	F. Boagey
G. Oliver	J.R. Wilkinson
R. (Bob) Taylor	C.W. Westerdale
H. Garrett	F. Bielby
J.E. Wyburn	G. Van Rooyen

Halftime: 8-3   Ref: F. Renton (Hunslet)   Att: 20,000 (£1,175)

29th September 1923 — N.R.F.L.

HULL	7	v	ROVERS	14

E. Rogers	L. Osborne *4 Goals*
W.H. Stone	L. Harris
J.E. Kennedy *2 Goals*	J. Cook
A.E. Bateson	R. Rees
T.E. Gwynne	G. Austin
S. Whitty	J. Hoult
E. Caswell *1 Try*	J. McIntyre
J. Beasty	J.H. Wilkinson *1 Try*
W. Brennan	F. Boagey
H. Bowman	J.R. Wilkinson
C. Ellery	F. Bielby *1 Try*
E. Morgan	C.W. Westerdale
H. Garrett	G. Van Rooyen

Halftime: 7-2   Ref: R. Robinson (Bradford)   Att: 16,468 (£974.5.0)

21st April 1923 — Championship Semi Final

HULL	2	v	ROVERS	16

E. Rogers	L. Osborne *2 Goals*
W.H. Stone	L. Harris
J.E. Kennedy *1 Goal*	R. Rees
W. Batten	J. Cook
J. Holdsworth	G. Austin *2 Tries*
T.E. Gwynne	J. Hoult *1 Try*
E. Caswell	J. McIntyre
H. Bowman	J.H. Wilkinson
G. Oliver	F. Boagey
J. Beasty	J.R. Wilkinson
J.E. Wyburn	C.W. Westerdale *1 Try*
E. Morgan	F. Bielby
H. Garrett	A. Moore

Halftime: 2-10   Ref: F. Renton (Hunslet)   Att: 28,000 (£1,644)

25th December 1923 — N.R.F.L.

ROVERS	18	v	HULL	9

L. Osborne *3 Goals*	E. Rogers
L. Harris	W.H. Stone
R. Rees	T. Collins
J. Hoult *1 Try*	W. Batten
G. Austin *1 Try*	T.E. Gwynne *3 Tries*
W. Clark	S. Whitty
J. McIntyre	E. Caswell
J.H. Wilkinson	J. Beasty
F. Boagey *(sent off)*	W. Brennan
J.R. Wilkinson	H. Bowman
C.W. Westerdale *(sent off)*	E. Morgan
A. Moore *1 Try*	R. (Bob) Taylor
H. Binks *1 Try*	H. Garrett

Halftime: 5-0   Ref: H. Swift (Halifax)   Att: 20,000 (£934)

4th October 1924 — N.R.F.L.

ROVERS	39	v	HULL	2

L. Osborne *5 Goals*		E. Jenney
L. Harris *2 Tries*		W.H. Stone
J. Cook *1 Try*		J.E. Kennedy *1 Goal*
J. Hoult *3 Tries*		T. Collins
G. Austin *1 Try; 1 Goal*		W.H. Dickinson
C.A. Webb		E. Caswell
J. McIntyre *1 Try*		T. McGiever
B. Britton		J. Beasty
F. Boagey *1 Try*		S. Pickering
J.R. Wilkinson		R.W. Bolderson
H. Binks		G. Howlett
C.W. Westerdale		G. Todd
A. Moore		A.E. Bateson

Halftime: Not known   Ref: R. Jones (Widnes)
Rec: (£822)

3rd October 1925 — N.R.F.L.

ROVERS	8	v	HULL	2

G. Austin *1 Goal*		E. Jenney
L. Harris		R. Garvey
J. Cook *1 Try*		J.E. Kennedy *1 Goal*
J. Hoult		W.J. Davies
W.H. Rhoades *1 Try*		T. Collins
J. Raynor		S. Whitty
J. McIntyre		E. Caswell
J.H. Wilkinson		H. Bowman
F. Boagey		S. Pickering
J.R. Wilkinson		J. Beasty
A. Carmichael		E. Morgan
F. Bielby		R. (Bob) Taylor *(sent off)*
C.W. Westerdale		A.E. Bateson

Halftime: 2-0   Ref: Mr. Fairbank (Wigan)   Att: 16,000

25th December 1924 — N.R.F.L.

HULL	4	v	ROVERS	4

E. Rogers		L. Osborne *2 Goals*
J. Cowan		L. Harris
J.E. Kennedy *2 Goals*		J. Cook
T. Collins		J. Hoult
W.H. Stone		G. Austin
S. Whitty		C.A. Webb
E. Caswell		J. McIntyre
J. Beasty		J.R. Wilkinson
S. Pickering		F. Boagey
E. Morgan		B. Britton
R. (Bob) Taylor		A. Carmichael
A.E. Bateson		F. Bielby
H. Longbottom		A. Moore

Halftime: 4-2   Ref: R. Jones (Widnes)   Att: 21,000 (£1,250)

25th December 1925 — N.R.F.L.

HULL	9	v	ROVERS	4

E. Jenney		L. Osborne *2 Goals*
T.E. Gwynne		G.W. Bateman
H. Atkinson		J. Cook
W.J. Davies		L. Harris
T. Collins		G. Austin
S. Whitty *1 Try*		J. Hoult
E. Caswell		J. McIntyre
H. Bowman		J.H. Wilkinson
S. Pickering		F. Boagey
J. Beasty		B. Britton
E. Morgan		C.W. Westerdale
R. (Bob) Taylor *2 Tries*		H. Binks
A.E. Bateson		F. Bielby

Halftime: 3-2   Ref: J. Eddom (Swinton)   Att: 20,500
(£1066.3.9)

25th December 1926 — N.R.F.L.

HULL	3	v	ROVERS	2

J. Higo	L. Osborne *1 Goal*
T. Collins	G.W. Bateman
W.J. Davies	J. Cook
H. Beardshaw	L. Harris
T.E. Gwynne	G. Austin
S. Whitty	J. Hoult
E. Caswell	J. McIntyre
H. Bowman *1 Try*	J.R. Wilkinson
S. Pickering	F. Boagey
J. Beasty	J.H. Wilkinson
R. (Bob) Taylor	C.W. Westerdale
J. Smallwood	B. Britton
A.E. Bateson	J. Feetham

Halftime: 3-2   Ref: H. Swift (Halifax)   Att: 20,000 (£1,160)

26th December 1927 — N.R.F.L.

HULL	2	v	ROVERS	2

E. Jenney *1 Goal*	L. Osborne *1 Goal*
J. Gardiner	G.W. Bateman
W.J. Davies	J. Spamer
S. Whitty	J. Cook
T.E. Gwynne	G. Austin
E. Caswell	J. Hall
J. Phillipson	J. McIntyre
H. Bowman	J.R. Wilkinson
R.W. Bolderson	H. Binks
M.G. Short	C.W. Westerdale
J.T. Smallwood	J. Feetham
A.E. Bateson	B. Britton
H. Longbottom	A. Carmichael

Halftime: 2-2   Ref: F. Peel (Bradford)   Att: 16,000 (£799.10.6)

15th April 1927 — N.R.F.L.

ROVERS	14	v	HULL	5

L. Osborne *1 Goal*	E. Jenney
L. Harris	T. Collins
J. Cook	W.J. Davies
J. Spamer *1 Try*	H. Beardshaw *1 Try*
G. Austin *1 Try*	T.E. Gwynne
G. Saul	S. Whitty
J. McIntyre	E. Caswell
J.R. Wilkinson	H. Bowman
F. Boagey	S. Pickering
J.H. Wilkinson *1 Try*	R.W. Bolderson
C.W. Westerdale	J.T. Smallwood
F. Bielby	R. (Bob) Taylor
J. Feetham *1 Try*	A.E. Bateson *1 Goal*

Halftime: 8-5   Ref: R. Robinson (Bradford)   Att: 17,500 (£1,018)

6th April 1928 — N.R.F.L.

ROVERS	11	v	HULL	5

L. Osborne *4 Goals*	E. Jenney
G.W. Bateman	J. Gardiner
J. Spamer	S. Whitty
J. Cook	W.J. Davies
A. Scarborough	T.E. Gwynne
G. Saul	J. Phillipson
J. McIntyre	E. Caswell
C.W. Westerdale	H. Bowman
H. Binks	R.W. Bolderson
J.R. Wilkinson	M.G. Short
J. Feetham *1 Try*	G. Howlett
G.E. Saddington	J.T. Smallwood
F. Roberts	A.E. Bateson *1 Try; 1 Goal*

Halftime: 9-5   Ref: F. Peel (Bradford)   Att: 14,000 (£855)

25th December 1928 — N.R.F.L.

HULL	2	v	ROVERS	6

E. Jenney	L. Osborne
R. Harsley	G.W. Bateman
W.J. Davies	J. Cook
J. Oliver	A.J. Jordan
T.E. Gwynne	J. Spamer *1 Try*
S. Whitty	H. Dale *1 Try*
Wilson Hall	J. McIntyre
R.W. Bolderson	H. Binks
S. Pickering	L. Sharpe
M.G. Short	B. Britton
H. Bowman	G.E. Saddington
J.T. Smallwood	C.W. Westerdale
A.E. Bateson *1 Goal*	J. Feetham

Halftime: 0-6   Ref: R. Robinson (Bradford)   Att: 14,000 (£772)

11th May 1929 — Friendly
(Benefit Match for J. Beasty/J.E. Kennedy)

HULL	25	v	ROVERS	10

E. Jenney *5 Goals*	G. Carmichael *1 Goal*
R.G. Everitt *1 Try*	J. Spamer *1 Try*
M. Eastburn	A. Scarborough
H. Lyon	J. Feetham
Sharp *1 Try*	F. Roberts
J. Phillipson	J. Hoult *1 Try; 1 Goal*
Wilson Hall *1 Try*	J. McIntyre
M.G. Short	C.W. Westerdale
S. Pickering	L. Sharpe
H. Bowman *2 Tries*	F. Westerdale
H. Longbottom	G.E. Saddington
S. Errington	H. Binks
A. Carmichael	F. Brindle

Halftime: 15-10   Ref: C.W. Eastman (Hull)   Att: 4,000

29th March 1929 — N.R.F.L.

ROVERS	3	v	HULL	9

L. Osborne	E. Jenney
G.W. Bateman *1 Try*	W.J. Davies
J. Cook	H. Lyon
A.J. Jordan	J. Oliver *3 Goals*
A. Scarborough	T.E. Gwynne *1 Try*
H. Dale	J. Phillipson
J. McIntyre	E. Caswell
B. Britton	M.G. Short
L. Sharpe	S. Pickering
H. Binks	H. Bowman
G.E. Saddington	A.E. Bateson
C.W. Westerdale	H. Longbottom
J. Feetham	A. Carmichael

Halftime: 0-4   Ref: R. Robinson (Bradford)   Att: 13,000 (£800)

25th December 1929 — N.R.F.L.

HULL	2	v	ROVERS	2

E. Jenney	L. Osborne *1 Goal*
H. Lyon	G.W. Bateman
W.J. Courtney	A.J. Jordan
J. Oliver *1 Goal*	J. Cook
T.E. Gwynne	J. McIntyre
E. Caswell	H. Dale
W.J. Davies	J. Spamer
H. Bowman	B. Britton
S. Pickering	L. Sharpe
G. Howlett	F. Roberts
S. Errington	H. Binks
M. Eastburn	C.W. Westerdale
A. Carmichael	H. Williams

Halftime: 2-0   Ref: R. Robinson (Bradford)   Att: 10,000
(£628.15.0)

18th April 1930 — N.R.F.L.

ROVERS	3	v	HULL	11

L. Osborne		E. Jenney
G.W. Bateman		T.E. Gwynne
R.W. Rhoades		W.J. Davies
A.J. Jordan		J. Oliver *4 Goals*
G. Carmichael *1 Try*		F. Winsor
J. McIntyre		E. Caswell
J. Spamer		W.A. Mills *1 Try*
B. Britton		H. Bowman
W. Jones		M.G. Short
C.W. Westerdale		F.H. Thompson
H. Binks		A.E. Bateson
L. Sharpe		G. Howlett
H. Williams		G.E. Wray

Halftime: 0-11   Ref: R. Robinson (Bradford)   Att: Not known
Rec: (£650)

3rd April 1931 — N.R.F.L.

ROVERS	11	v	HULL	5

L. Osborne *1 Goal*		E. Jenney
G. Carmichael *1 Try*		G.W. Bateman *1 Try*
J. Spamer		J. Oliver *1 Goal*
W. Batten *1 Try*		S. Whitty
J. McIntyre		F. Winsor
H. Dale		W. Mills
J. Parkin		W. Metcalf
B. Britton *1 Try*		H. Bowman
H. Binks		Adamson
C.W. Westerdale		F.H. Thompson
G.E. Saddington		H. Ellerington
L. Sharpe		F. Wood
F. Brindle		A.E. Bateson

Halftime: 3-5   Ref: E. Robinson (Bradford)   Att: 11,000

25th December 1930 — N.R.F.L.

HULL	8	v	ROVERS	0

E. Jenney *1 Goal*		G. Carmichael
G.W. Bateman *2 Tries*		C. Rainton
J. Oliver		J. Spamer
H. Lyon		R. Hill
R. Harsley		F. Roberts
J. Phillipson		J. Parkin
E. Caswell		J. McIntyre
H. Bowman		B. Britton
Adamson		H. Binks
F.H. Thompson		L. Sharpe
A.E. Bateson		G.E. Saddington
S. Errington		F. Brindle
A. Carmichael		F. Westerdale

Halftime: 5-0   Ref: R. Robinson (Bradford)   Att: 16,000 (£832)

25th December 1931 — N.R.F.L.

HULL	0	v	ROVERS	10

H. Lyon		G. Carmichael *2 Goals*
G.W. Bateman		H. Williams
J. Oliver		W. Batten
C.R. Fifield		J. McIntyre
F. Winsor		C. Rainton
J. Ashton		H. Dale
W. Metcalf		J. Parkin *1 Try*
S. Errington		B. Britton
S. Pickering		H. Binks
F.H. Thompson		L. Sharpe *1 Try*
H. Bowman		G.E. Saddington
F. Wood		C.W. Westerdale
A. Carmichael		F. Brindle

Halftime: 0-7   Ref: H. Horsfall (Batley)   Att: 14,000 (£871)

October 1964. Jim Drake gets his pass in before being tackled by Jim Neale and Clive Sullivan. Rovers' Poole streaked down the left for a try. The "Robins" won 23-9. Photo by courtesy of Hull Daily Mail.

The Hull F.C. team which went down 31-5 at Craven Park in April 1966. Back row (left to right) McGlone, Pearson, C. Booth, R. Booth, Sykes, Macklin, Oliver, Stocks. Front row: Foulkes, Maloney, Keegan, Devonshire, Doyle-Davidson. Photo by courtesy of Hull Daily Mail.

20th February 1932 — Friendly

HULL	14	v	ROVERS	10

W. Teall	L. Osborne
G.W. Bateman *1 Try*	E. McCloud
J. Oliver *1 Try; 1 Goal*	J. Spamer *2 Goals*
C.R. Fifield	G. Carmichael *1 Try*
H. Lyon *1 Try*	W. Batten *1 Try*
R.G. Everitt	H. Dale
H. Ellerington	W. McWatt
S. Errington	B. Britton
S. Pickering	H. Binks
F.H. Thompson	F. Blossom
A. Carmichael	L. Sharpe
W. Stead *1 Try*	G.E. Saddington
W.J. Courtney	F. Brindle

Halftime: 5-2   Ref: J. McEwan (York)   Att: 1,000

14th April 1933 — N.R.F.L.

HULL	5	v	ROVERS	7

W. Teall	G. Carmichael *2 Goals*
G.W. Bateman *1 Try*	J. Edmonds
J. Oliver *1 Goal*	J. Spamer *1 Try*
C.R. Fifield	J. Smith
F. Winsor	W. Batten
W. Metcalf	H. Dale
H. Ellerington	R. Fridlington
F.H. Thompson	F. Blossom
C. Wilkinson	H. Binks
H. Bowman	W. Eddoms
W. Stead	G.E. Saddington
G. Barlow	J.W. Moores
A. Carmichael	H. Williams

Halftime: 2-7   Ref: B. Laughlin (Batley)   Att: 15,000
(£605.17.9)

25th March 1932 — N.R.F.L.

ROVERS	7	v	HULL	2

L. Osborne	W. Teall *1 Goal*
R. Hill	G.W. Bateman
J. Spamer	J. Oliver
W. Batten	C.R. Fifield
G. Carmichael *1 Try; 2 Goals*	H. Lyon
H. Dale	H. Ellerington
J. Parkin	R.G. Everitt
B. Britton	F.H. Thompson
H. Binks	S. Pickering
F. Blossom	W. Stead
L. Sharpe	H. Bowman
G.E. Saddington	A. Carmichael
F. Brindle	W.J. Courtney

Halftime: 7-0   Ref: F. Peel (Bradford)   Att: 11,000
(£628.6.2)

29th April 1933 — N.R.F.L.

ROVERS	3	v	HULL	0

G. Carmichael	W. Teall
J. Edmonds	F. Winsor
J. Spamer	J. Sowerby
R. Hill	J. Oliver
W. Batten *1 Try*	Richardson
H. Dale	W. Metcalf
R. Fridlington	C.R. Fifield
B. Britton	F.H. Thompson
H. Binks	C. Wilkinson
W. Eddoms	H. Bowman
G.E. Saddington	W. Stead
E. Tattersfield	G. Barlow
J.W. Moores	G.E. Mathers

Halftime: 3-0   Ref: F. Peel (Bradford)   Att: Not known

16th September 1933 — N.R.F.L.

ROVERS	8	v	HULL	24

G. Carmichael *1 Goal*	W. Teall
J. Woodcock	G.W. Bateman *1 Try*
J. Spamer	J. Oliver *1 Try; 6 Goals*
R. Hill	J. Sowerby
A. Wood	F. Winsor *1 Try*
A. Lewis *1 Try*	C.R. Fifield *1 Try*
H. Dale *1 Try*	J. Phillipson
F. Blossom	H. Bowman
H. Binks	C. Wilkinson
W. Eddoms	Thames
G.E. Saddington	W. Stead
L. Sharpe	L. Thacker
H. Williams	A. Carmichael

Halftime: 2-12   Ref: J. Orford (Wigan)   Att: 10,000

25th December 1934 — N.R.F.L.

HULL	26	v	ROVERS	12

F. Miller *3 Goals*	T.H. Shipp
G.W. Bateman	R. Hill
J. Oliver *2 Tries; 1 Goal*	J. Spamer
C.R. Fifield *1 Try*	H. Beaumont *2 Goals*
R. Corner	W. Batten *1 Try*
F. Colling	H. Dale *1 Try*
E. Herberts *2 Tries*	J. Eastwood
A. Carmichael	F. Shillito
G. Barlow	J. Ramsden
W. Stead	L. Clarke
L. Barlow	L. Beaumont
J.R.P. Dawson	E. Tattersfield *1 Goal*
H. Ellerington *1 Try*	H. Williams

Halftime: 15-9   Ref: F. Peel (Bradford)   Att: 15,000

30th March 1934 — N.R.F.L.

HULL	22	v	ROVERS	14

F. Miller *4 Goals*	G. Carmichael *4 Goals*
G.W. Bateman *1 Try*	G. Deeley
J. Oliver *1 Try*	J. Spamer *1 Try*
C.R. Fifield	H. Walshaw
R. Corner *1 Try*	J. Eastwood
F. Colling	J. Woodcock
E. Herberts *1 Try; 1 Goal*	H. Beaumont
H. Bowman	F. Blossom
C. Wilkinson	W. Eddoms
L. Thacker	H. Binks
W. Stead	C. Brown
G. Barlow	A. Jackson
A. Carmichael	H. Williams *1 Try*

Halftime: 6-5   Ref: F. Peel (Bradford)   Att: 16,000

19th April 1935 — N.R.F.L.

ROVERS	10	v	HULL	17

W. McWatt *2 Goals*	F. Miller *1 Goal*
F. Winsor	G.W. Bateman *2 Tries*
J. Spamer	J. Oliver *3 Goals*
H. Walshaw *1 Try*	C.R. Fifield
A. Lewis	R. Corner *1 Try*
T. McGowan	E. Herberts
A. Moss	F. Colling
F. Riach	A. Carmichael
J. Ramsden	G. Barlow
F. Thompson	W. Stead
F. Shillito	J.R.P. Dawson
E. Tattersfield *1 Try*	L. Barlow
J.W. Moores	H. Ellerington

Halftime: 2-15   Ref: J. Eddoms (Swinton)   Att: 20,000

9th May 1935 — Friendly (Great War Trust Fund Shield)

HULL	12	v	ROVERS	12
F. Miller			W. McWatt	
T. Fletcher *1 Try*			A. Wood *1 Try*	
J. Oliver *1 Try*			C. Rainton	
J. Sowerby			J. Spamer	
W. Sheard *1 Try*			J. Sherburn *2 Tries*	
F. Colling			H. Dale	
W.J. Courtney			T. McGowan *1 Try*	
A. Carmichael			F. Shillito	
G. Barlow			J. Ramsden	
W. Stead			F. Thompson	
J.R.P. Dawson			E. Tattersfield	
L. Barlow *1 Try*			L. Clarke	
H. Ellerington			F. Brindle	

Halftime: 9-9   Ref: G. Tomes (York)   Att: 2,100

10th April 1936 — N.R.F.L.

HULL	12	v	ROVERS	2
F. Miller			W. McWatt *1 Goal*	
S. Wilson			F. Winsor	
J. Oliver *3 Goals*			J. Spamer	
C.R. Fifield			G. Whitton	
R. Corner			A. Wood	
W.J. Courtney *1 Try*			J. Eastwood	
E. Herberts			H. Dale	
W. Stead			F. Shillito	
G. Barlow			J. Ramsden	
L. Thacker			F. Thompson *(sent off)*	
C. Booth (Snr) *1 Try*			W. Eddoms	
J.R.P. Dawson			E. Tattersfield	
H. Ellerington			G.E. Saddington	

Halftime: Not known Ref: J.E. Taylor (Wakefield)   Att: 20,000

25th December 1935 — N.R.F.L.

ROVERS	5	v	HULL	15
G. White			F. Miller *1 Goal*	
A. Wood *1 Try*			C. Gouldstone *2 Tries*	
W. McWatt *1 Goal*			J. Oliver *1 Try; 2 Goals*	
J. Spamer			C.R. Fifield	
J. Eastwood			R. Corner	
G. Whitton			E. Herberts	
H. Beaumont			W.J. Courtney	
W. Eddoms			W. Stead	
J. Ramsden			G. Barlow	
F. Thompson			L. Thacker	
F. Shillito			J.R.P. Dawson	
E. Tattersfield			L. Barlow	
L. Beaumont			H. Ellerington	

Halftime: 2-8   Ref: J.E. Taylor (Wakefield)   Att: 15,000

12th September 1936 — Yorkshire Cup (1st Round)

ROVERS	13	v	HULL	17
W. McWatt *2 Goals*			F. Miller	
H. Beaumont			S. Wilson	
J. Eastwood			J. Oliver *1 Try; 4 Goals*	
G. Whitton			C.R. Fifield	
A. Wood *1 Try*			R. Corner	
V. Young *2 Tries*			E. Herberts	
J. Phillips			W.J. Courtney	
W. Eddoms			W. Stead *1 Try*	
J. Ramsden			G. Barlow *1 Try*	
R. Maskill			L. Thacker	
E. Tattersfield			J.R.P. Dawson	
L. Beaumont			L. Barlow	
J. Cayzer			G.E. Mathers	

Halftime: 10-10   Ref: P. Cowell (Warrington)   Att: 15,000

25th December 1936 — N.R.F.L.

HULL	6	v	ROVERS	3

F. Miller	W. McWatt
E. Overton	W. Perrott
J. Oliver *3 Goals*	N. Foster
S. Wilson	J. Spamer
R. Corner	J. Eastwood *1 Try*
W.J. Courtney	H. Beaumont
T.A. Johnson	V. Young
L. Thacker	R. Maskill
L. Murray	J. Ramsden
L. Barlow	F. Thompson
J.R.P. Dawson	L. Beaumont
C. Booth (Snr)	J. Cayzer
H. Ellerington	E. Tattersfield

Halftime: 6-0   Ref: J.E. Taylor (Wakefield)   Att: 20,000 (£900)

25th December 1937 — N.R.F.L.

ROVERS	5	v	HULL	27

G. White	F. Miller
A. Harrison	F. Hurley *3 Tries*
J. Spamer	J. Oliver *1 Try; 3 Goals*
W. McWatt *1 Goal*	S. Wilson *1 Try*
J. Eastwood	R. Corner *1 Try*
T. McGowan	W.J. Courtney
S. Morgan	T.A. Johnson
F. Shillito *1 Try*	L. Thacker
J. Ramsden	G. Barlow
R. Maskill	L. Barlow
J. McNulty	C. Booth (Snr)
L. Beaumont	J.R.P. Dawson *1 Try*
F. Middleton	H. Ellerington

Halftime: 2-13   Ref: A. Hill (Leeds)   Att: 17,000 (£730)

26th March 1937 — N.R.F.L.

ROVERS	8	v	HULL	14

W. McWatt *1 Goal*	F. Miller *2 Goals*
G. Whitton	R.W. Davies
N. Foster	J. Oliver *2 Goals*
J. Spamer	C.R. Fifield
J. Eastwood *2 Tries*	S. Wilson *1 Try*
T. McGowan	E. Herberts
H. Dale	W.J. Courtney
R. Maskill	L. Thacker
J. Ramsden	G. Barlow
F. Thompson	L. Barlow
F. Middleton	J.R.P. Dawson *1 Try*
L. Beaumont	C. Booth (Snr)
J. Cayzer	H. Ellerington

Halftime: 2-5   Ref: F. Peel (Bradford)   Att: 20,000 (£970)

15th April 1938 — N.R.F.L.

HULL	12	v	ROVERS	13

F. Miller *3 Goals*	W. McWatt
F. Hurley	H. Beaumont
S. Wilson *1 Try*	B. Hutchinson *1 Try*
R. Corner	J. Oliver *2 Goals*
W. Dockar	J. Eastwood
T.A. Johnson	S. Morgan *1 Try*
E. Herberts *1 Try*	H. Dale
L. Thacker	F. Shillito
G. Barlow	J. Ramsden
L. Barlow	R. Maskill
E. Wray	L. Beaumont *1 Try*
C. Booth (Snr)	L. Clarke
H. Ellerington	J. Cayzer

Halftime: 5-10   Ref: A. Hill (Leeds)   Att: 25,000 (£1,100)

26th December 1938 — N.R.F.L.

HULL	5	v	ROVERS	2

F. Miller *1 Goal*	G. White
F. Hurley	J. Spamer
A.E. Allen	J. Oliver
S. Brogden	W. McWatt *1 Goal*
W. Goodall	H. Beaumont
E. Herberts *1 Try*	S. Morgan
T.A. Johnson	J. Eastwood
L. Thacker	L. Beaumont
G. Barlow	R. Maskill
W.J. Morrell	L. Blanchard
C. Booth (Snr)	L. Clarke
J.R.P. Dawson	R. Moxon
H. Ellerington	J. Cayzer

Halftime: 0-2   Ref: A.S. Dobson (Featherstone)   Att: 9,000 (£417)

7th April 1939 — N.R.F.L.

ROVERS	14	v	HULL	4

W. McWatt *1 Goal*	F. Miller *2 Goals*
J. Spamer *1 Try*	W. Dockar
J. Eastwood *2 Tries*	A.E. Allen
W. Perrott	S. Wilson
J.C. Milner	A. Bowers
J. Naylor	E. Herberts
S. Morgan	T.A. Johnson
R. Maskill	L. Thacker
J. Ramsden	G. Barlow
L. Blanchard	W.J. Morrell
L. Clarke	C. Booth (Snr)
L. Beaumont	J.R.P. Dawson
J. Cayzer *1 Try*	E. Wray

Halftime: 6-2   Ref: A.S. Dobson (Featherstone)   Att: 13,000 (£605)

4th February 1939 — R.L. Cup (1st Round)

ROVERS	8	v	HULL	5

G. White	F. Miller *1 Goal*
J. Spamer *1 Try*	F. Hurley
J. Oliver	A.E. Allen
W. McWatt *1 Goal*	S. Brogden
J.C. Milner	A. Bowers
J. Eastwood	E. Herberts
S. Morgan	T.A. Johnson
R. Maskill	L. Thacker
J. Ramsden	G. Barlow
L. Blanchard	W.J. Morrell
L. Clarke	C. Booth (Snr)
L. Beaumont *1 Try*	J.R.P. Dawson *1 Try*
J. Cayzer	H. Ellerington

Halftime: 5-5   Ref: A.E. Harding (Broughton)   Att: 22,000

23rd September 1939 — Friendly

HULL	22	v	ROVERS	8

F. Miller *4 Goals*	W. McWatt
W. Dockar *2 Tries*	B. Hutchinson
A.E. Allen	J. Spamer
A. Bowers	J. Eastwood
E. Overton *1 Try*	W. Beaumont *2 Tries*
J. Bilton	J. Naylor
H. Mills *1 Try*	R. Mills
G.E. Mathers	R. Maskill
G. Barlow *1 Try*	J. Ramsden
J. Tindall	L. Blanchard
C. Booth (Snr) *1 Try*	L. Clarke
R. Kavanagh	Boxall *1 Goal*
H. Bedford	A. Dockar

Halftime: 8-3   Ref: E. Willis (Hull)   Att: 6,000

Hull's Chris Davidson hangs on to Rovers' John Moore in December 1967. Rovers won 15-9. Photo by courtesy of Hull Daily Mail.

Ian Madley. Photo by courtesy of Hull Daily Mail.

Phil Edmonds. Photo by courtesy of Hull Daily Mail.

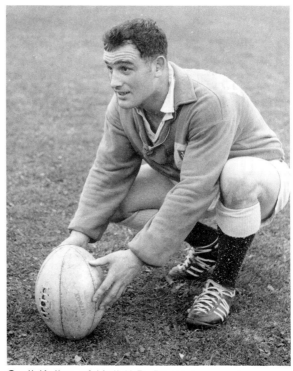

Cyril Kellett of Hull K.R. Photo by courtesy of Hull Daily Mail.

25th December 1939 — War League

HULL	11	v	ROVERS	10

F. Miller *1 Goal*	G. Carmichael *(Bradford) 2 Goals*
W. Dockar	J. Spamer
A.E. Allen	F. Brindle *(Castleford)*
H. Mills	W. McWatt
A. Bowers *2 Tries*	R. Moxon *1 Try*
E. Lawrence	Kaye
T.A. Johnson	M. Daddy
G.A. Pinder	L. Blanchard
H. Wilkinson	J. Ramsden
G.E. Mathers	L. Clarke
C. Booth (Snr)	E. Bedford
J.R.P. Dawson *1 Try*	E. Tattersfield
R. Kavanagh	A. Dockar *1 Try*

Halftime: 11-10   Ref: A.S. Dobson (Featherstone)   Att: 8,000

25th December 1945 — N.R.F.L.

HULL	25	v	ROVERS	9

B. Spamer *2 Goals*	W. McWatt
T. Glynn *4 Tries*	H. Gee *1 Try*
A. Bowers	H. Bratley
I. Watts *2 Tries*	W. Beaumont
Jeffries	J. Eastwood
E. Lawrence	S. Morgan
H. Crane	W. Ness
S. Hattersley	L. Clarke
H. Wilkinson	J. Ramsden
J. Tindall *1 Try*	V. Hill
C. Booth (Snr)	S. Atkinson *2 Tries*
E. Wray	E. Bedford
J. Holt	B. Goldswain

Halftime: 11-3   Ref: A.S. Dobson (Featherstone)   Att: 15,000

26th December 1939 — War League

ROVERS	7	v	HULL	14

W. Teall *(Wakefield) 2 Goals*	F. Miller *1 Goal*
J. Spamer *1 Try*	W. Dockar
W. McWatt	A.E. Allen
G. Carmichael *(Bradford)*	H. Mills *3 Tries*
F. Brindle *(Castleford)*	A. Bowers
Kaye	E. Lawrence
M. Daddy	T.A. Johnson *1 Try*
L. Blanchard	G.A. Pinder
W. Eddoms	S. Hattersley
L. Clarke	G. Beales
E. Bedford	C. Booth (Snr)
E. Tattersfield	J.R.P. Dawson
A. Dockar	G.E. Mathers

Halftime: 5-8   Ref: J.E. Taylor (Wakefield)   Att: 6,000 (£115)

At the end of the 1939 - 40 season, Hull Kingston
Rovers decided to cease activities for the duration
of the War. They recommenced in 1945 - 46.

19th April 1946 — N.R.F.L.

ROVERS	23	v	HULL	9

W. McWatt *4 Goals*	B. Spamer *3 Goals*
J. Nicholls *1 Try*	Jeffries
B. Goldswain	I. Watts
E. Bedford	A. Bowers
W. Beaumont	T. Glynn
W. Ness	E. Lawrence
R. Mills	E. Smailes
L. Clarke	L. Thacker
J. Ramsden *2 Tries*	S. Sweeting
V. Hill	F.W. Shillito
P. Wilmot	C. Booth (Snr)
S. Atkinson	J. Tindall *1 Try*
A. Dockar *2 Tries*	S. Hattersley

Halftime: 5-2   Ref: A.S. Dobson (Featherstone)   Att: 16,000 (£1,226)

10th October 1946 — Yorkshire Cup (Semi Final)

HULL	15	v	ROVERS	11

F. Miller *3 Goals*	W. McWatt *1 Goal*
T. Glynn	H. Gee
I. Watts *2 Tries*	B. Goldswain
A.D. Sinclair	G. Megson
A. Bowers	W. Beaumont
E. Lawrence *1 Try*	R. Mills *1 Try*
T.A. Johnson	E. Richards *2 Tries*
F.W. Shillito	V. Hill
H. Wilkinson	J. Ramsden
S. Jimmison	L. Hartley
C. Booth (Snr)	S. Atkinson
J. Tindall	P. Wilmot
A. Shakesby	A. Dockar

Halftime: 2-8   Ref: E. Devine (Leeds)   Att: 15,000

4th April 1947 — N.R.F.L.

ROVERS	17	v	HULL	13

W. McWatt	F. Miller *2 Goals*
F. McBain *2 Tries*	L. Sanders
H. Mills	A.D. Sinclair
M. Daddy	J. Sullivan
W. Beaumont *1 Try*	A. Bowers *1 Try*
E. Richards	E. Lawrence
R. Mills *4 Goals*	T. Glynn
A. Senior	P. Fallon
J. Ramsden	A. Noble
V. Hill	J. Tindall *2 Tries*
S. Atkinson	A. Bedford
B. Goldswain	S. Hattersley
A. Dockar	R. Kavanagh

Halftime: 8-3   Ref: Not known   Att: 14,000 (£1,100)

25th December 1946 — N.R.F.L.

HULL	9	v	ROVERS	5

F. Miller *3 Goals*	W. McWatt *1 Goal*
T. Glynn	F. McBain
A.D. Sinclair	H. Mills
J. Sullivan	J. Barraclough
A. Bowers	W. Beaumont
E. Lawrence	R. Mills
R. Jewitt	E. Richards *1 Try*
F.W. Shillito	L. Hartley
S. Hattersley *1 Try*	J. Ramsden
P. Fallon	A. Senior
C. Booth (Snr)	B. Goldswain
A. Bedford	S. Atkinson
A. Shakesby	A. Dockar

Halftime: 4-5   Ref: Not known   Att: 14,000 (£1,100)

The Club's first all-ticket match

25th December 1947 — N.R.F.L.

ROVERS	9	v	HULL	5

M. Daddy	F. Miller *1 Goal*
E. Richards *2 Tries*	A. Bowers
C. Smith	A.D. Sinclair
W. Jackson *1 Try*	J. Sullivan
F. McBain	B. Ryan
C. Steele	E. Lawrence
R. Mills	R. Jewitt *1 Try*
A. Senior	S. Jimmison
J. Ramsden	G. Watt
G. Barker	C. Booth (Snr)
S. Atkinson	A. Bedford
B. Goldswain	J. Tindall
A. Dockar	E.R. Davies

Halftime: 0-0   Ref: A.S. Dobson (Featherstone)   Att: 15,000 (£1,170)

26th March 1948 — N.R.F.L.

HULL	0	v	ROVERS	8

F. Miller	W. McWatt *1 Goal*
A. Bowers	J. Scofield
A.D. Sinclair	J. Barraclough
B. Madden	W. Jackson
B. Ryan	F. McBain *1 Try*
E. Lawrence	H. Mills
R. Jewitt	R. Mills *1 Try*
R. Kavanagh	A. Palframan (Jnr)
G. Watt	J. Ramsden
C. Booth (Snr)	G. Barker
E. Bedford	P. Wilmot
J. Tindall	B. Goldswain
H. Evans	A. Dockar

Halftime: 0-0   Ref: Not known   Att: 22,600 (£1,810)

15th April 1949 — N.R.F.L.

ROVERS	7	v	HULL	4

W. McWatt *2 Goals*	T. Hart *2 Goals*
E. Richards	L. Sanders
C. Smith	C. Turner
H. Mills	J. Sullivan
J. Chapman	K. Gittoes
C. Steele	E. Lawrence
L. Oates	D. Jackson
P. Wilmot	T. Danter
J. Ramsden	G. Watt
H. Welsby	J. Tindall
J. Barraclough	W. Jones
D. Scholes *1 Try*	J. Payne
A. Dockar	A.D. Sinclair

Halftime: 0-2   Ref: Not known   Att: 14,000 (£1,300)

25th December 1948 — N.R.F.L.

HULL	15	v	ROVERS	0

T. Hart *3 Goals*	W. McWatt
B. Madden *1 Try*	E. Richards
A.D. Sinclair	C. Smith
J. Sullivan	H. Mills
B. Ryan *1 Try*	J. Schofield
E. Lawrence	R. Mills
D. Jackson	C. Steele
T. Danter	P. Wilmot
G. Watt	J. Ramsden
C. Booth (Snr)	A. Palframan (Jnr)
B. Poole	W. Welsby
A. Bedford	B. Goldswain
H. Evans *1 Try*	A. Dockar

Halftime: 7-0   Ref: A. Hemmings (Halifax)   Att: 15,000

26th December 1949 — N.R.F.L.

ROVERS	9	v	HULL	0

J. Lewis *3 Goals*	T. Hart
G. Tullock	K. Gittoes
A. Ferguson *1 Try*	C. Turner
P. Clark	B. Nicklin
A. Payne	B. Ryan
H. Mills	I. Watts
M. Daddy	D. Burnell
A. Palframan (Jnr)	T. Danter
J. Ramsden	G. Watt
G. Barker	W. Jones
D. Scholes	A. Bedford
J. Barraclough	B. Poole
A. Dockar	M. Scott

Halftime: 4-0   Ref: W. Hemmings (Halifax)   Att: 16,000 (£1,270)

7th April 1950 — N.R.F.L.

HULL	15	v	ROVERS	6

T. Hart *3 Goals*	J. Lewis *3 Goals*
L. Sanders *3 Tries*	G. Tullock
C. Turner	H. Mills
I. Watts	A. Payne
B. Ryan	P. Clark
E. Lawrence	G. Tate
D. Jackson	L. Oates
T. Danter	A. Palframan (Jnr)
G. Watt	J. Ramsden
C. Booth (Snr)	G. Barker
M. Scott	J. Barraclough
B. Poole	D. Scholes
A. Bedford	L. Clark

Halftime: 8-6   Ref: J. Jackson (Barrow)   Att: 18,000

25th December 1950 — N.R.F.L.

HULL	3	v	ROVERS	3

T. Hart	P. Ingram
K. Gittoes	G. Tullock
I. Watts	W. Cornforth
R. Francis *1 Try*	H O'Connor
E. Walters	G. Tate *1 Try*
E. Lawrence	B. Spence
D. Jackson	R. Mills
T. Danter	A. Palframan (Jnr)
P.T. Harris	S. Smith
D. Foreman	G. Young
L. Baxter	J. Barraclough
A. Bedford	F. Moore
J. Whiteley	A. Dockar

Halftime: 3-3   Ref: M. Coates (Pudsey)   Att: 13,000

12th May 1950 — Friendly
(Play off for Jack Townend Memorial Trophy)

HULL	12	v	ROVERS	7

T. Hart *3 Goals*	J. Lewis *2 Goals*
L. Sanders *2 Tries*	G. Tullock
B. Nicklin	H. Lewis
S. Shaw	H. Mills
I. Watts	G. Tate
E. Lawrence	C. Steele
D. Jackson	J. Nicholls
T. Danter	A. Palframan (Jnr)
P.T. Harris	J. Ramsden
S. Jimmison	S. Smith
B. Poole	J. Barraclough
A. Bedford	D. Scholes *1 Try*
H. Evans	A. Dockar

Halftime: 4-2   Ref: R. Gelder (Wakefield)   Att: 8,000 (£588)

23rd March 1951 — N.R.F.L.

ROVERS	21	v	HULL	4

P. Ingram	T. Hart *1 Goal*
G. Tullock *1 Try*	I. Watts
H. Lewis	C. Hutton
R. Mills	E. Walters
W. Cornforth *1 Try*	R. Francis
B. Spence	G. Cox
M. Daddy *1 Try*	C. Knapp
G. Young	D. Foreman *1 Goal*
S. Smith	P.T. Harris
F. Moore *1 Try*	J. Clark
J. Barraclough	A. Bedford
D. Scholes *1 Try*	M. Scott
A. Dockar *3 Goals*	J. Whiteley

Halftime: 13-2   Ref: G.S. Phillips (Widnes)   Att: 12,000 (£946)

25th December 1951 — N.R.F.L.

ROVERS	10	v	HULL	18

T. Sutton	T. Hart *3 Goals*
G. Tullock	K. Gittoes *1 Try*
R. Mills *4 Goals*	C. Hutton
D. Rushton	R. Francis *1 Try*
G. Warters	I. Watts *1 Try*
J. McAvoy	B. Conway
P. Armitage *1 Goal*	D. Burnell *1 Try*
A. Palframan (Jnr)	M. Scott
J. Tong	P.T. Harris
A. Dockar	R. Coverdale
W.G. Forth	A. Bedford
J. Barraclough	J. Drake
D. Turner	J. Whiteley

Halftime: 8-8   Ref: R. Welsby (Warrington)   Att: 13,500 (£1,001)

25th December 1952 — N.R.F.L.

HULL	9	v	ROVERS	16

T. Hart *3 Goals*	D. Briggs
G. Cox	G. Tullock
C. Hutton	D. Rushton
C. Turner	J. McAvoy *2 Tries*
R. Francis *1 Try*	T. Sutton
B. Conway	R.B. Knowelden
A. Tripp	M. Daddy
W. Hopkins	A. Palframan (Jnr)
P.T. Harris	S. Smith
R. Coverdale	F. Moore
H. Markham	D. Turner
M. Scott	M. Anderson
J. Whiteley	A. Dockar *5 Goals*

Halftime: 9-4   Ref: J.W. Jackson (Barrow)   Att: 11,000 (£1,010)

11th April 1952 — N.R.F.L.

HULL	9	v	ROVERS	5

T. Hart	J. McAvoy
R. Francis *1 Try*	G. Tullock
C. Hutton	H. Mills
J. Whiteley	R.B. Knowelden
I. Watts	W. Egan
B. Conway	H. Lewis
D. Burnell *1 Try*	P. Armitage
M. Scott	G. Young
P.T. Harris *1 Try*	J. Tong
R. Coverdale	G. Barker
J. Drake	M. Anderson
H. Markham	D. Turner *1 Try*
A. Bedford	A. Dockar *1 Goal*

Halftime: 3-5   Ref: F. Smith (Barrow)   Att: 18,500

3rd April 1953 — N.R.F.L.
(Played at Boothferry Park, Hull)

ROVERS	2	v	HULL	13

D. Chalkley *1 Goal*	J. Watkinson
G. Tullock	I. Watts
D. Rushton	R. Francis
J. McAvoy	C. Hutton *2 Goals*
J. Moore	G. Cox *1 Try*
R.B. Knowelden	C. Turner
M. Daddy	A. Tripp
A. Palframan (Jnr)	M. Scott
S. Smith	P.T. Harris
J. Tong	R. Coverdale
D. Turner	N. Hockley
M. Anderson	H. Markham
A. Dockar	J. Whiteley *2 Tries*

Halftime: 0-5   Ref: G.S. Phillips (Widnes)   Att: 27,670 (£3,280)

Anxiety as Rovers' Australian forward, Arthur Beetson, has broken his leg in the 1968 Christmas Day Derby at Craven Park. Photo by courtesy of Hull Daily Mail.

Christmas Day Derby 1968. David Doyle-Davidson makes a break for Hull, with Phil Lowe covering. Rovers won 9-0. Photo by courtesy of Hull Daily Mail.

21st September 1953 — N.R.F.L.
(Played at Boothferry Park, Hull)

ROVERS	4	v	HULL	15

T. Buckle *2 Goals*	J. Watkinson
A. Garry	K. Bowman
J. Barraclough	W. Riches
G. Tullock	C. Turner *3 Goals*
E. Knapp	J.W. Staples
R.B. Knowelden	B. Conway
B. Beck	A. Tripp
A. Palframan (Jnr)	M. Scott
S. Smith	P.T. Harris
F. Moore	R. Coverdale
J. Tong	H. Markham *2 Tries*
S. Evans	N. Hockley
M. Anderson	A. Bedford *1 Try*

Halftime: 4-6   Ref: G.S. Phillips (Widnes)   Att: 16,720 (£1,976)

25th December 1954 — N.R.F.L.

HULL	16	v	ROVERS	6

C. Hutton *2 Goals*	P. O'Leary
I. Watts	D.Rushton *1 Try*
C. Turner	P. Austin
R. Francis	B. Beck *1 Try*
W. Coulman	A. Garry
B. Conway	T. Buckle
T. Finn *1 Try*	J. Parker
M. Scott	K. Harbour
P.T. Harris *1 Try*	J. Tong
R. Coverdale	K. Grice
H. Markham *1 Try*	F. Moore
N. Hockley	T. Sutton
J. Whiteley *1 Try*	D. Turner

Halftime: 8-3   Ref: M. Coates (Pudsey)   Att: 8,500 (£771)

25th December 1953 — N.R.F.L.

HULL	32	v	ROVERS	2

C.Hutton *4 Goals*	T. Buckle
K. Bowman	A. Garry
W. Riches	D. Turner
R. Francis	G. Tullock
I. Watts *4 Tries*	D. Rushton
B. Conway *1 Try*	M.Thornton
A. Tripp *1 Try*	B. Beck *1 Goal*
M. Scott *1 Try*	A. Palframan (Jnr)
P.T. Harris	S. Smith
R. Coverdale *1 Try*	K. Harbour
A. Bedford	J. Holt
H. Markham	M. Anderson
J. Whiteley	T. Sutton

Halftime: 18-2   Ref: G.S. Phillips (Widnes)   Att: 12,500 (£1,020)

8th April 1955 — N.R.F.L.
(Played at Boothferry Park, Hull)

ROVERS	5	v	HULL	13

P. O'Leary	C. Hutton *2 Goals*
B. Golder	K. Bowman *2 Tries*
K. Goulding	D. Brindle
P. Austin	C. Turner *1 Try*
A. Garry	I. Watts
T. Buckle *1 Goal*	B. Conway
J. Parker	T. Finn
F. Moore	M. Scott
J. Tong	P.T. Harris
K. Harbour	R. Coverdale
G. Tullock *1 Try*	H. Markham
T. Sutton	N. Hockley
J. Shires	J. Whiteley

Halftime: 2-7   Ref: G.S. Phillips (Widnes)   Att: 17,155 (£2,124)

8th October 1955 — N.R.F.L.
(Played at Boothferry Park, Hull)

ROVERS	21	v	HULL	20

T. Buckle	C. Hutton *4 Goals*
B. Golder	K. Bowman
K. Goulding *1 Try*	B. Cooper
A. Bartliffe	W. Riches *1 Try*
A. Garry	I. Watts *1 Try*
M. Thornton	R. Moat *1 Try*
J. Parker *1 Goal*	T. Finn
K. Grice *1 Try*	M. Scott *1 Try*
J. Tong	P.T. Harris
S. Evans *5 Goals*	J. Drake
J. Hall	H. Markham
J. Shires *1 Try*	W. Drake
T. Sutton	J. Whiteley

Halftime: 9-4   Ref: J.W. Jackson (Barrow)   Att: 16,670
(£1,911.2.0)

1st October 1956 — N.R.F.L.
(Played at Boothferry Park, Hull)

ROVERS	5	v	HULL	16

T. Buckle *1 Goal*	C. Hutton *5 Goals*
J. Chapman	K. Bowman
N. Hancock	B. Cooper
B. Coulson	J. Whiteley
A. Garry	I. Watts
P. Key	C. Turner
B. Beck	T. Finn *1 Try*
J. Hall *1 Try*	M. Scott *1 Try*
J. Tong	P.T. Harris
B. Croft	J. Drake
T. Bourton	H. Markham
D. Johnson	W. Drake *(sent off 50min)*
J. Shires	C. Sykes

Halftime: 5-7   Ref: E. Clay (Leeds)   Att: 18,742 (£2,260)

30th March 1956 — N.R.F.L.

HULL	27	v	ROVERS	9

C. Hutton *6 Goals*	T. Buckle *3 Goals*
K. Bowman *3 Tries*	B. Shaw
B. Cooper	N. Hancock *(sent off 60min)*
C. Turner	M. Thornton
K. Gittoes	A. Garry
R. Moat	J. Parker
T. Finn *(sent off 1st half)*	P. Key
M. Scott	K. Grice
P.T. Harris *1 Try*	L. Brookfield
R. Coverdale	B. Croft
H. Markham	T. Bourton
W. Drake *1 Try*	T. Sutton
J. Whiteley	D. Smith *1 Try*

Halftime: 7-9   Ref: A. Howgate (Dewsbury)   Att: 18,000 (£1,669)

25th December 1956 — N.R.F.L.

HULL	30	v	ROVERS	2

C. Hutton *3 Goals*	T. Buckle *1 Goal*
W. Coulman	B. Shaw
S. Cowan	N. Hancock
C. Turner *1 Try*	B. Coulson
I. Watts *4 Tries*	A. Garry
R. Moat *2 Tries*	P. Key
T. Finn *1 Try*	G. Coulson
M. Scott	T. Danter
P.T. Harris	J. Tong
J. Drake	S. Evans
H. Markham	B. Croft
W. Drake	J. Hall
J. Whiteley	C. Harper

Halftime: 3-2   Ref: R.L. Thomas (Oldham)   Att: 12,500
(£1210.16.0)

7th October 1957 — N.R.F.L.
(Played at Boothferry Park, Hull)

ROVERS	0	v	HULL	21

G. Coulson	P. Bateson *3 Goals*
G. Garton	S. Cowan *2 Tries*
C. Kellett	B. Saville *1 Try*
B. Coulson	C. Turner
B. Shaw	G. Dannatt
P. Key	F. Broadhurst
R. Evans	T. Finn *1 Try*
K. Grice	M. Scott
R. Walters	P.T. Harris
S. Evans	J. Drake *1 Try*
T. Sutton	B. Hambling
A. Matthews	C. Hutton
P. Bangs	J. Whiteley

Halftime: 0-15   Ref: A. Howgate (Dewsbury)   Att: 20,156 (£2,476)

25th December 1958 — N.R.F.L.

HULL	11	v	ROVERS	2

P. Bateson *4 Goals*	C. Kellett *1 Goal*
R. Gill	E. Wilson
B. Saville	W. Riley
S. Cowan	R. Moat
I. Watts	B. Coulson
G. Matthews	P. Key
T. Finn	D. Elliott
M. Scott	J. Rogers
P.T. Harris	L. Brookfield
B. Hambling	D. Holland
C. Sykes	D. Scholes
W. Drake	J. Taylor
J. Whiteley *1 Try*	K. Jacques

Halftime: 6-2   Ref: G. Phillpott (Leeds)   Att: 16,000 (£1,560)

4th April 1958 — N.R.F.L.

HULL	15	v	ROVERS	8

P. Bateson *3 Goals*	G. Fishwick *1 Goal*
G. Dannatt	B.Coulson
B. Cooper	W. Riley
B. Saville *1 Try*	J. Mageen *1 Try*
I. Watts *1 Try*	B.Shaw *1 Try*
F. Broadhurst	P. Key
T. Finn	R. Evans
M. Scott	K. Grice
P.T. Harris	L. Brookfield
J. Drake	R. Coverdale
B. Hambling	D. Holland
W. Drake *1 Try*	H. Griffett
J. Whiteley	D. Scholes

Halftime: 7-3   Ref: N.T. Railton (Wigan)   Att: 27,000 (£2,690)

21st March 1959 — R.L. Cup (3rd Round)

HULL	23	v	ROVERS	9

P. Bateson *4 Goals*	C. Kellett *3 Goals*
S. Cowan	B. Coulson *1 Try*
B. Cooper	W. Riley
R. Boustead *2 Tries*	P. Key
I. Watts	R. Moat
G. Matthews	G. Paul
T. Finn	D. Elliott
M. Scott	K. Grice
P.T. Harris	A. Ackerley
J. Drake *1 Try*	D. Holland
P. Whiteley	J. Jenkin
W. Drake	K. Jacques
J. Whiteley *2 Tries*	J. Taylor

Halftime: 5-4   Ref: T.W. Watkinson (Manchester)   Att: 24,000

27th March 1959 — N.R.F.L.
(Played at Boothferry Park, Hull)

ROVERS	**12**	v	**HULL**	**24**

C. Kellett *3 Goals*	P. Bateson *6 Goals*
B. Coulson	S. Cowan *2 Tries*
W. Riley	B. Cooper
G. Garton	B. Saville
R. Moat	I. Watts
G. Paul *1 Try*	G. Matthews
P. Key *1 Try*	T. Finn
D. Holland	M. Scott
J. Keegan	P.T. Harris
J. Rogers	B. Hambling
J. Jenkin	P. Whiteley
K. Jacques	W. Drake
J. Taylor	J. Whiteley *2 Tries*

Halftime: 9-13   Ref: A.E. Durkin (Dewsbury)   Att: 21,594 (£2,744)

25th April 1960 — N.R.F.L.

HULL	**17**	v	**ROVERS**	**4**

P. Bateson *4 Goals*	T. Major
T. Devonshire *1 Try*	B. Coulson
S. Cowan	W. Riley
G. Harrison *1 Try*	Joe Drake
D. Johnson	W. Coulman
F. Broadhurst	G. Paul
T. Finn *1 Try*	D. Elliott
M. Scott	K. Grice
P.T. Harris	A. Ackerley
S. Evans	R. Coverdale
T. Sutton	K. Kingsbury *2 Goals*
W. Drake	G. Hackling
J. Whiteley	C. Last

Halftime: 8-4   Ref: G. Philpott (Leeds)   Att: 22,000 (£1,937)

25th December 1959 — N.R.F.L.

ROVERS	**2**	v	**HULL**	**13**

C. Kellett *1 Goal*	P. Bateson *2 Goals*
G. Paul	S. Cowan
B. Coulson	B. Saville *1 Try*
W. Riley	J. Kershaw *1 Try*
W. Coulman	E. Wanklyn *1 Try*
A. Burwell	G. Matthews
A. Bunting	T. Finn
R. Rowbottom	M. Scott
A. Ackerley	P.T. Harris
R. Coverdale	J. Drake
J. Jenkin	C. Sykes
R. Speckman	W. Drake
K. Farnhill	J. Whiteley

Halftime: 0-4   Ref: E. Clay (Leeds)   Att: 12,000 (£1,200)

6th August 1960 — Eva Hardaker Memorial Trophy

HULL	**16**	v	**ROVERS**	**26**

C. Ali	C. Kellett *7 Goals*
T. Devonshire *1 Try*	B. Coulson
G. Harrison *1 Try*	T. Major *1 Try*
S. Cowan *1 Try*	Joe Drake
E. Wanklyn	R. Harris *1 Try*
F. Broadhurst	G. Paul
T. Finn	D. Elliott *(A. Bunting 1 Try)*
W. Drake	R. Coverdale
R. Walters	A. Ackerley
J. Drake	E. Thundercliffe
C. Sykes *2 Goals*	R. Jacques *1 Try*
M. Smith *1 Try*	K. Kingsbury
J. Whiteley	J. Taylor

Halftime: 6-14   Ref: G. Wilson (Dewsbury)   Att: 8,000 (£750)

12th November 1960 — N.R.F.L.

HULL	13	v	ROVERS	2

P. Bateson *2 Goals*	C. Kellett *1 Goal*
D. Johnson *1 Try*	G. Paul
S. Cowan *1 Try*	W. Riley
B. Saville	A. Mullins
T. Hollindrake *1 Try*	R. Moat
G. Matthews	A. Bunting
J. Smith	D. Elliott
M. Scott	M. Kirk
P.T. Harris	P. Flanagan
J. Drake	R. Coverdale
C. Sykes	K. Kingsbury
W. Drake	J. Jenkin
J. Whiteley	R. Jacques

Halftime: 8-2   Ref: L. Gant (Wakefield)   Att: 12,800 (£1,167)

17th April 1961 — N.R.F.L.

ROVERS	14	v	HULL	10

A. Mullins	J. Kershaw
G. Paul *2 Tries*	D. Doyle-Davidson
B. Matthews	G. Matthews
C. Kellett *4 Goals*	S. Cowan
B. Shaw	T. Hollindrake *1 Try*
D. Elliott	F. Broadhurst
A. Bunting	T. Finn
R. Coverdale	M. Scott
P. Flanagan	J. Drake
B. Tyson	B. Hambling
A. Thompson	C. Sykes
J. Taylor	W. Drake *1 Try; 2 Goals*
H. Poole	J. Whiteley

Halftime: 10-5   Ref: G. Wilson (Dewsbury)   Att: 13,000 (£1,430)

25th February 1961 — R.L. Cup (2nd Round)

HULL	16	v	ROVERS	3

P. Bateson *5 Goals*	C. Kellett
G. Matthews	G. Paul *1 Try*
J. Kershaw	T. Major
B. Saville	A. Mullins
T. Hollindrake	R. Harris
F. Broadhurst	B. Matthews
T. Finn *1 Try*	A. Bunting
M. Scott	R. Coverdale
P.T. Harris	P. Flanagan
J. Drake *1 Try*	B. Tyson
C. Sykes	J. Taylor
W. Drake	C. Trowell
J. Whiteley	H. Poole

Halftime: 2-0   Ref: R. Gelder (Wakefield)   Att: 17,000 (£1,695)

12th August 1961 — Eva Hardaker Memorial Trophy

ROVERS	14	v	HULL	5

C. Kellett *4 Goals*	P. Bateson *1 Goal*
G. Paul	S. Cowan
B. Matthews	G. Matthews
A. Burwell	B. Saville
R. Harris *1 Try*	T. Hollindrake
D. Elliott	F. Broadhurst *1 Try*
A. Bunting *1 Try*	T. Finn
B. Tyson	M. Scott
P. Flanagan	P.T. Harris
J. Jenkin	J. Drake
J. Taylor	B. Hambling
H. Poole	M. Storey
E. Bonner	W. Drake

Halftime: 2-5   Ref: L. Gant (Wakefield)   Att: 9,000

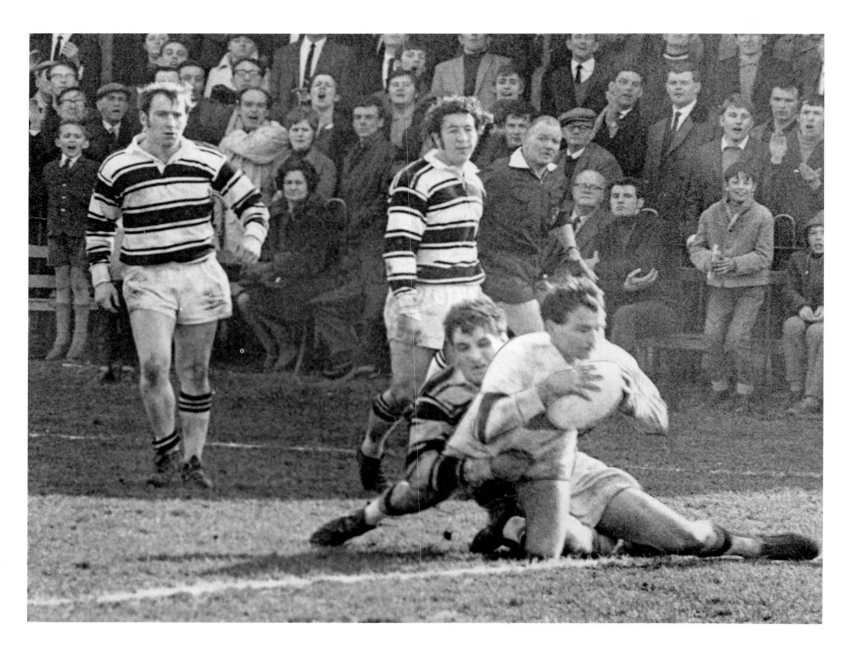

Alan Burwell scores for Rovers, despite Harrison's tackle, as Rovers win 29-9, April 1969. Photo by courtesy of Hull Daily Mail.

Clive Sullivan, M.B.E.

Phil Lowe, Hull K.R.
Photo by courtesy of Hull Daily Mail.

During the Summer of 1962, Hull and Rovers undertook a tour of Cornwall to stage a series of exhibition games in an attempt to expand the game in that part of the country.

16th September 1961 — N.R.F.L.

ROVERS	13	v	HULL	12

C. Kellett *2 Goals*	P. Bateson *3 Goals*
T. Stocks *2 Tries*	J. Kershaw
T. Major *1 Try*	R. Gemmell
B. Burwell	T. Hollindrake *1 Try*
A. Mullins	K. Barnwell
B. Matthews	G. Matthews
A. Bunting	F. Broadhurst
R. Coverdale	B. Hambling
A. Holdstock	P.T. Harris
B. Tyson	J. Drake
A. Thompson	C. Sykes *1 Try*
H. Poole	M. Smith
E. Bonner	B. Clixby

Halftime: 3-4   Ref: A. Durkin (Dewsbury)   Att: 12,750

17th February 1962 — N.R.F.L.

HULL	7	v	ROVERS	9

A. Keegan	C. Kellett *3 Goals*
W. Rosenberg	R. Harris
R. Gemmell	T. Major
T. Hollindrake *2 Goals*	B. Burwell
C. Sullivan	G. Paul
J. Kershaw *1 Try*	D. Elliott
T. Finn	A. Bunting
M. Scott	R. Coverdale
I. Corban	A. Ackerley
B. Hambling	J. Drake
W. Drake	B. Tyson
C. Booth (Jnr)	E. Bonner *1 Try*
M. Smith	H. Poole

Halftime: 4-4   Ref: M. Coates (Pudsey)   Att: 18,000 (£1,600)

4th June 1962 (at Penzance)

HULL	57	v	ROVERS	26

A. Keegan *6 Goals*	C. Kellett *4 Goals*
T. Devonshire *3 Tries*	G. Paul *1 Try*
R. Gemmell *2 Tries*	B. Burwell *1 Try*
T. Hollindrake *3 Tries; 2 Goals*	M. Blackmore
J. Kershaw	T. Stocks
G. Matthews *2 Tries; 1 Goal*	D.Elliott *(Sub: B. Hatch 1 Try)*
T. Finn *1 Try*	A. Bunting *1 Try*
M. Scott	R. Coverdale
B. Clixby	A. Lockwood
W. Drake *1 Try*	J. Drake
C. Booth (Jnr)	A. Thompson
M. Smith *1 Try*	B. Tyson *2 Tries*
C. Sykes	E. Palmer

Ref: C.F. Appleton (Warrington)   Att: 2,300

5th June 1962 (at Camborne)

HULL	38	v	ROVERS	26

A. Keegan *7 Goals*	C. Kellett *4 Goals*
T. Devonshire *2 Tries*	G. Paul
D. Doyle-Davidson *1 Try*	A. Mullins
T. Hollindrake *2 Tries*	T. Stocks
K. Barnwell *3 Tries*	B. Burwell
G. Matthews	A. Bunting *1 Try*
T. Finn	B. Hatch *2 Tries*
M. Scott	P. Murphy *1 Try*
B. Clixby	P. Flanagan
W. Drake	J. Drake
C. Booth (Jnr)	A. Thompson *1 Try*
M. Smith	B. Tyson *1 Try*
C. Sykes	H. Poole

Re: C.F. Appleton (Warrington)   Att: 1,500

6th June 1962 (at Falmouth)

HULL	44	v	ROVERS	29

A. Keegan	C. Kellett *5 Goals*
T. Devonshire *3 Tries*	G. Paul *1 Try*
R. Gemmell *2 Tries; 1 Goal*	P. Murphy
T. Hollindrake *1 Try; 5 Goals*	A. Mullins *1 Try*
K. Barnwell *2 Tries*	B. Burwell
G. Matthews	A. Bunting
T. Finn	B. Hatch *1 Try*
M. Scott	R. Coverdale
J. Macklin	P. Flanagan
W. Drake *1 Try*	J. Drake
C. Booth (Jnr)	A. Thompson *2 Tries*
M. Smith	B. Tyson
C. Sykes *1 Try; 1 Goal*	H. Poole *2 Tries*

Ref: C.F. Appleton (Warrington) Att: 2,000

20th August 1962 — Eastern Division

ROVERS	19	v	HULL	5

C. Kellett *5 Goals*	A. Keegan *1 Goal*
G. Paul	T. Devonshire
T. Major	R. Gemmell
B. Burwell	T. Hollindrake
R. Harris *1 Try*	K. Barnwell *1 Try*
D. Elliott	G. Matthews
B. Hatch	K. McGowan
K. Grice	M. Scott
P. Flanagan *1 Try*	I. Corban
J. Drake	W. Drake
P. Murphy *1 Try*	T. Whitehead
B. Tyson	C. Booth (Jnr)
E. Bonner	M. Smith

Halftime: 14-5 Ref: L. Wingfield (Normanton) Att: 8,800

11th August 1962 — Eva Hardaker Memorial Trophy

HULL	28	v	ROVERS	11

A. Keegan *5 Goals*	C. Kellett *4 Goals*
W. Rosenberg *2 Tries*	G. Paul
R. Gemmell	T. Major
T. Hollindrake *2 Tries*	T. Stocks
C. Sullivan	R. Harris *1 Try*
J. Kershaw	D. Elliott
T. Finn	A. Bunting
T. Whitehead	K. Grice
B. Clixby	A. Lockwood
M. Storey	R. Coverdale
C. Sykes *1 Try*	K. Farnhill
C. Booth (Jnr) *1 Try*	P. Murphy
J. Whiteley	A. Thompson

Halftime: 10-6 Ref: C. Whiteley (Ossett) Att: 9,500

1st September 1962 — Eastern -Division

HULL	9	v	ROVERS	24

A. Keegan *3 Goals*	C. Kellett *3 Goals*
W. Rosenberg	G. Paul *2 Tries*
R. Gemmell	T. Major *1 Try*
T. Hollindrake	M. Blackmore *1 Try*
G. Matthews *1 Try*	R. Harris
T. Devonshire	D. Elliott *1 Try*
K. McGowan	B. Hatch
T. Whitehead	K. Grice
I. Corban	P. Flanagan
W. Drake	J. Drake
M. Storey	B. Tyson *1 Try*
C. Booth	E. Bonner
B. Clixby	H. Poole

Halftime: 7-11 Ref: D.S. Brown (Dewsbury) Att: 14,000

12th April 1963 — Division One

ROVERS	4	v	HULL	2

C. Kellett *2 Goals*	A. Keegan *1 Goal*
G. Paul	W. Rosenberg
T. Major	R. Gemmell
M. Blackmore	T. Hollindrake
R. Harris	C. Sullivan
D. Elliott	C. Nimb
A. Bunting	T. Finn
R. Coverdale	M. Scott
P. Flanagan	R. Walters
J. Drake	N. Hockley
B. Tyson	M. Storey
L. Chamberlain	C. Sykes
J. Taylor	B. Clixby

Halftime: 4-2   Ref: H. Pickersgill (Castleford)

Att: 14,400 (Ground Post War Record) (£1,701)

17th August 1963 — Eva Hardaker Memorial Trophy

ROVERS	11	v	HULL	15

L. Clark *1 Goal*	A. Keegan *3 Goals*
G. Paul *2 Tries*	W. Rosenberg
B. Burwell	R. Gemmell
M. Blackmore *1 Try*	C. Nimb
R. Harris	C. Sullivan
D. Elliott	T. Devonshire *2 Tries*
B. Hatch	T. Finn
R. Coverdale	W. Drake
A. Lockwood	R. Walters
B. Tyson	J. Macklin
J. Taylor	C. Booth (Jnr)
H. Poole	M.Storey *1 Try*
L. Chamberlain	F. Johnson

Halftime: 8-5   Ref: P. Geraghty (York)   Att: 9,000

8th May 1963 — Division One

HULL	5	v	ROVERS	19

A. Keegan *1 Goal*	C. Kellett *5 Goals*
W. Rosenberg	G. Paul *1 Try*
R. Gemmell	T. Major *1 Try*
T. Hollindrake *1 Try*	M. Blackmore
B. Sullivan	R. Harris *1 Try*
T. Devonshire	D. Elliott
T. Finn	A. Bunting
W. Drake	R. Coverdale
R. Walters *(sent off)*	A. Lockwood *(sent off)*
N. Hockley	P. Fox
C. Sykes	B. Tyson
M. Storey	E. Bonner
P. Whiteley	L. Clarke

Halftime: 5-7   Ref: G. Philpott (Leeds)   Att: 15,000 (£1,570)

14th December 1963 — Division One

ROVERS	24	v	HULL	2

E. McNamara	A. Keegan *1 Goal*
G. Paul	W. Rosenberg
T. Major	T. Carmichael
A. Burwell *2 Tries*	T. Hollindrake
R. Harris *1 Try*	B. Sullivan
D. Elliott	T. Devonshire
A. Bunting *1 Try*	T. Finn
F. Fox	N. Hockley
P. Flanagan *1 Try*	A. McGlone
B. Tyson	R. Booth
L. Clark *3 Goals*	J. Macklin
H. Poole	C. Sykes
J. Taylor *1 Try*	P. Whiteley

Halftime: 11-2   Ref: G. Philpott (Leeds)   Att: 7,050 (£652)

27th March 1964 — Division One

HULL	5	v	ROVERS	13

A. Keegan *1 Goal*	C. Kellett *2 Goals*
W. Rosenberg	G. Paul *1 Try*
G. Stocks	T. Major
T. Carmichael	J. Moore
C. Mountain	M. Blackmore *1 Try*
D. Doyle-Davidson	A. Burwell
T. Finn	D. Elliott
T. Casey	B. Tyson
A. McGlone	P. Flanagan
C. Sykes	J. Taylor
J. Neale	E. Palmer
E. Broom *1 Try*	L. Clark *1 Try*
F. Johnson	H. Poole

Halftime: 5-5   Ref: G. Wilson (Dewsbury)   Att: 11,500 (£1,297)

17th October 1964 — N.R.F.L.

ROVERS	23	v	HULL	9

C. Kellett *7 Goals*	A. Keegan *1 Try*
R. Harris	B. Sullivan
T. Major	K. Barnwell
J. Moore	G. Stocks
M. Blackmore	T. Devonshire
A. Burwell *1 Try*	K. Huxley
A. Bunting	K. Foulkes
J. Bath	J. Macklin
P. Flanagan	A. McGlone
J. Drake	R. Booth
B. Tyson	J. Neale
J. Taylor *1 Try*	E. Broom *3 Goals*
H. Poole *1 Try*	J. Whiteley

NPS: D. Elliott – L. Clark   NPS: T. Carmichael – C. Sykes

Halftime: 14-7   Ref: L. Gant (Wakefield)   Att: 12,000

15th August 1964 — Eva Hardaker Memorial Trophy

HULL	14	v	ROVERS	35

A. Keegan *4 Goals*	C. Kellett *2 Tries; 7 Goals*
B. Sullivan *1 Try*	C. Young
G. Stocks	J. Moore
T. Carmichael	M. Blackmore
C. Sullivan	R. Harris *2 Tries*
K. Huxley	A. Burwell *1 Try*
K. McGowan *1 Try*	B. Hatch
J. Macklin	J. Bath *2 Tries*
A. McGlone	A. Holdstock
R. Booth	B. Tyson
J. Whiteley	E. Bonner
J. Neale	J. Taylor
A.N. Other	H. Poole

Halftime: 7-20   Ref: E. Clay (Leeds)   Att: 8,500

16th April 1965 — N.R.F.L.

HULL	12	v	ROVERS	10

A. Keegan	C. Kellett *5 Goals*
B. Sullivan	A. Mullins
G. Stocks	B. Burwell
D. Doyle-Davidson *1 Try*	J. Moore
C. Sullivan	M. Blackmore *(sent off 65min)*
T. Devonshire *1 Try*	D. Elliott
K. Foulkes	C. Cooper
G. Pearson	F. Fox
A. McGlone	P. Flanagan
E. Broom *3 Goals*	W. Holliday
J. Neale	L. Clark
K. Owens	F. Foster
C. Sykes	H. Poole

NPS: J. Brown – F. Johnson   NPS: N. Gillard – J. Bath

Halftime: 7-8   Ref: D.S. Brown (Dewsbury)   Att: 16,500

The Rugby League decided to allow substitutes from August 1964, up to two in number for injured players up to the start of the second half. Subsequently, various alterations to the rules regarding substitutes have been implemented. Playing substitutes are indicated in brackets following the player they replace. Non-playing substitutes are indicated by NPS.

16th August 1965 — Eva Hardaker Memorial Trophy

ROVERS	11	v	HULL	6

C. Kellett *2 Goals*	A. Keegan
G. Paul	G. Stocks
T. Major	D. Doyle-Davidson
J. Moore	T. Carmichael
M. Blackmore	C. Sullivan
D. Elliott *1 Try*	T. Devonshire
A. Bunting	K. Foulkes
J. Bath	G. Pearson
R. Holdstock	A. McGlone
K. Pollard	R. Booth
F. Foster	E. Broom *3 Goals*
W. Holliday *2 Goals*	M. Harrison
H. Poole	C. Sykes

Halftime: 7-4   Ref: J.P. Hebblethwaite (York)   Att: 12,000 (£1,465)

8th April 1966 — N.R.F.L.

ROVERS	31	v	HULL	5

C. Kellett *5 Goals*	A. Keegan
C. Young *1 Try*	N. Oliver
D. Elliott *2 Tries*	D. Doyle-Davidson
J. Moore *2 Tries*	J. Maloney *1 Goal*
M. Blackmore *1 Try*	G. Stocks
M. Stephenson	T. Devonshire *1 Try*
A. Bunting *1 Try*	K. Foulkes *(K. Huxley)*
F. Fox	G. Pearson
P. Flanagan	A. McGlone *(J. Edson)*
B. Tyson	J. Macklin
F. Foster	C. Booth (Jnr)
W. Holliday	R. Booth
T. Major	C.Sykes

NPS: A. Mullins – K. Pollard

Halftime: 23-0   Ref: E. Lawrenson (Warrington)   Att: 14,000 (£1,402)

25th December 1965 — N.R.F.L.

HULL	0	v	ROVERS	2

A. Keegan	A. Mullins
G. Stocks	C. Young
D. Doyle-Davidson	G. Wrigglesworth
J. Maloney	J. Moore
C. Sullivan	M. Blackmore
T. Devonshire	D. Elliott
K. McGowan	M. Stephenson
	(A. Bunting 40min)
G. Pearson	F. Fox
A. McGlone	P. Flanagan
E. Broom	B. Mennell
S. O'Brien	W. Holliday *1 Goal*
M. Harrison	G. Young *(K. Pollard 40min)*
J. Neale	F. Foster

NPS: K. Huxley – B. Clixby

Halftime: 0-2   Ref: J.P. Hebblethwaite (York)   Att: 8,500 (£1,262)

12th August 1966 — Eva Hardaker Memorial Trophy

HULL	2	v	ROVERS	27

D. Doyle-Davidson	C. Kellett *6 Goals*
N. Oliver	C. Young *1 Try*
K. Huxley *1 Goal*	G. Wrigglesworth
J. Maloney	J. Moore
C. Sullivan	M. Blackmore
C. Davidson	D. Elliott *(A. Bunting 1 Try)*
K. Foulkes	M. Stephensom *3 Tries*
S. O'Brien	F. Fox
A. McGlone *(B. Clixby)*	J. Shaw
J. Neale	B. Tyson
C. Booth	W. Holliday
M. Harrison	F. Foster *(E. Palmer)*
F. Johnson	T. Major

NPS: J. Brown

Halftime: 0-12   Ref: E. Clay (Leeds)   Att: 5,428

Rovers' new signing from Hull, Cyril Sykes, forces Alf Macklin to lose the ball in a tackle, and John Moore (left) scores a try, April 1971. Hull won 26-12 at the Boulevard. Photo by courtesy of Hull Daily Mail.

Hull F.C.'s Chairman, Charles Watson (left), with the Second Division Bowl and the Colts League Trophy, together with Hull K.R. Chairman, Bill Land, with the League Championship Trophy, all won in season 1978/79. Photo by courtesy of Hull Daily Mail.

3rd September 1966 — Yorkshire Cup (1st Round)

HULL	20	v	ROVERS	24

A. Keegan	C. Kellett *6 Goals*
N. Oliver *1 Try*	C. Young
D. Doyle-Davidson *1 Try*	A. Burwell
J. Maloney *4 Goals*	J. Moore *1 Try*
C. Sullivan *1 Try*	M. Blackmore *2 Tries*
K. Huxley	R. Millward
K. Foulkes	A. Bunting *1 Try*
M. Harrison	F. Fox
K. Owens *1 Try*	P. Flanagan
J. Edson	B. Tyson
S. O'Brien	W. Holliday
R. Morgan	F. Foster
C. Sykes	T. Major
NPS: Brown – C. Booth	*NPS: D. Elliott – E. Palmer*

Halftime: 10-17   Ref: E. Lawrenson (Warrington)   Att: 8,302 (£1,308)

1st April 1967 — N.R.F.L.

ROVERS	26	v	HULL	8

C. Kellett *5 Goals*	A. Keegan
C. Young *2 Tries*	N. Oliver
D. Elliott	D. Doyle-Davidson
J. Moore *1 Try*	*(C. Davidson)*
D. Wainwright	J. Maloney *4 Goals*
R. Millward *(M. Stephenson)*	K. Barnwell
A. Bunting	T. Devonshire
F. Fox	K. Foulkes *(D. Doyle-Davidson)*
P. Flanagan *1 Try*	M. Harrison
B. Tyson	A. McGlone
W. Holliday *1 Goal*	G. Pearson
T. Major	S. O'Brien
F. Foster	N. Trotter *(E. McNamara)*
NPS: P. Lowe	G. Stocks

Halftime: 5-8   Ref: R. Appleyard (Leeds)   Att: 10,600

24th March 1967 — N.R.F.L.

HULL	13	v	ROVERS	12

A. Keegan	D. Wainwright
N. Oliver *1 Try*	C. Young
D. Doyle-Davidson *1 Drop Goal*	A. Burwell *(D. Elliott)*
J. Maloney *4 Goals*	J. Moore
M. Lunn	S. Flannery *1 Try*
T. Devonshire	C. Cooper
K. Foulkes *(C. Davidson)*	M. Stephenson
M. Harrison	F. Fox
A. McGlone	P. Flanagan *1 Try*
E. Broom *(G. Pearson)*	B. Tyson
G. Stocks	W. Holliday *3 Goals*
N. Trotter	T. Major
C. Sykes	F. Foster
	NPS: P. Lowe

Halftime: 2-7   Ref: S. Shepherd (Oldham)   Att: 14,100 (£2,157)

15th August 1967 — Eva Hardaker Memorial Trophy

HULL	9	v	ROVERS	20

A. Keegan	D. Wainwright
N. Oliver	C. Young *1 Try*
D. Doyle-Davidson	A. Burwell *3 Tries*
J. Maloney	J. Moore *(A. Bunting)*
J. Brown *2 Tries*	A. Smith
T. Devonshire *1 Try*	R. Millward
C. Davidson	D. Elliott
M. Harrison	J. Taylor
A. McGlone	P. Flanagan
J. Neale	W. Holliday *4 Goals*
J. Macklin	P. Lowe
J. Edson	T. Major
G. Charlesworth	F. Foster
NPS: M. Lunn – C. Booth	*NPS: J. Hickson*

Halftime: 3-10   Ref: H. Cook (Beverley)   Att: 5,610 (£1,072)

18th September 1967 — BBC2 Floodlit Trophy
(Preliminary Round)

ROVERS	12	v	HULL	8
C. Kellett *2 Goals*			A. Keegan	
C. Young			N. Oliver *1 Try*	
J. Moore			D. Doyle-Davidson	
A. Burwell			J. Maloney *1 Goal*	
G. Ballantyne			G. Stocks	
R. Millward *(D. Elliott)*			T. Devonshire	
C. Cooper *1 Try*			C. Davidson *1 Try*	
W. Holliday *1 Goal*			M. Harrison	
P. Flanagan			A. McGlone	
J. Taylor			J. Macklin	
P. Lowe *1 Try*			N. Trotter	
J. Hickson			J. Edson	
T. Major			C. Sykes	
NPS: B. Mennell			*NPS: B. Hancock – S. O'Brien*	

Halftime: 6-5   Ref: H. Hunt (Prestbury)   Att: 14,280 (£2,568)

25th December 1967 — N.R.F.L.

HULL	9	v	ROVERS	15
A. Keegan			B. Cooper	
N. Oliver *1 Try*			C. Young	
B. Hancock			A. Burwell	
J. Maloney *3 Goals*			P. Longstaff	
C. Sullivan			P. Coupland	
T. Devonshire			J. Moore	
C. Davidson *(sent off 75mins)*			C. Cooper	
M. Harrison			W. Holliday *6 Goals*	
A. McGlone			P. Flanagan *1 Try*	
E. Broom			B. Mennell	
J. Neale			F. Foster	
J. Macklin			P. Lowe	
N. Trotter			T. Major	
NPS: J. Brown – C. Forster			*NPS: D. Elliott – A. Mullins*	

Halftime: 2-9   Ref: E. Clay (Leeds)   Att: 11,800 (£2,329)

14th October 1967 — Yorkshire Cup Final
(at Headingley)

HULL	7	v	ROVERS	8
A. KEEGAN			C. KELLETT *1 Goal*	
N. OLIVER			C. YOUNG	
D. DOYLE-DAVIDSON			J. MOORE	
J. MALONEY *1 Goal*			D. ELLIOTT	
G. STOCKS			A. BURWELL *1 Try*	
T. DEVONSHIRE			R. MILLWARD *1 Try*	
C. DAVIDSON *1 Try; 1 Goal*			C. COOPER	
M. HARRISON			W. HOLLIDAY	
A. McGLONE			P. FLANAGAN	
E. BROOM			B. MENNELL	
J. EDSON			J. HICKSON *(F. FOSTER 40min)*	
J. MACKLIN			P. LOWE	
C. SYKES			T. MAJOR	
NPS: B. HANCOCK –			*NPS: P. COUPLAND*	
G. CHARLESWORTH				

Halftime: 5-5   Ref: D. Davies (Manchester)   Att: 16,729 (£5,514)

12th April 1968 — N.R.F.L.

ROVERS	5	v	HULL	19
D. Wainwright			A. Keegan	
C. Young			N. Oliver	
J. Moore			J. Maloney *6 Goals*	
P. Longstaff *1 Try*			R. Gemmell	
B. Brook			C. Sullivan	
R. Millward			B. Hancock	
C. Cooper			C. Davidson *1 Try; 1 Drop Goal*	
L. Foster			M. Harrison	
P. Flanagan			A. McGlone	
B. Mennell			C. Forster	
W. Holliday *1 Goal*			J. Edson	
F. Foster			J. Neale	
P. Lowe			J. Brown *1 Drop Goal*	
NPS: A. Burwell – J. Hickson			*NPS: D. Doyle-Davidson*	
			S. O'Brien	

Halftime: 0-11   Ref: R.L. Thomas (Oldham)   Att: 14,720 (£2,475)

5th August 1968 — Eva Hardaker Memorial Trophy

HULL	20	v	ROVERS	21

A. Keegan	*4 Goals*	D. Wainwright	
C. Sullivan	*1 Try*	C. Young	
A. Macklin	*1 Try*	J. Moore	*2 Tries*
R. Gemmell	*1 Try*	A. Mead	
H. Firth	*1 Try*	P. Coupland	*2 Tries*
B. Hancock		B. Brook	
D. Doyle-Davidson		C. Cooper	
M. Harrison		L. Foster	
A. Duke		P. Flanagan	
S. O'Brien		J. Taylor	
J. Neale		P. Lowe	
J. Edson		W. Holliday	*3 Goals*
J. Brown		A. Mullins	

NPS: M. Owbridge – A.N. Other   NPS: J. Hickson – A Moran

Halftime: 15-9   Ref: J.P. Hebblethwaite (York)   Att: 5,895 (£1,491)

25th December 1968 — N.R.F.L.

ROVERS	9	v	HULL	0

D. Wainwright		A. Keegan	
C. Young		N. Oliver	
J. Moore		J. Maloney	
G. Wrigglesworth		D. Doyle-Davidson	
P. Longstaff		H. Firth	
M. Stephenson		B. Hancock	
C. Cooper		C. Davidson	
T. Clawson	*3 Goals*	M. Harrison	
P. Flanagan		R. Firth	
B. Mennell		J. Macklin	
P. Lowe		D. Jervis	*(C. Forster)*
A. Beetson	*(J. Hall)*	N. Trotter	
C. Wallis	*1 Try*	J. Brown	

NPS: B. Brook   NPS: A. Macklin

Halftime: 7-0   Ref: W.H. Thompson (Huddersfield)   Att: 10,000 (£1,820)

4th April 1969 — N.R.F.L.

HULL	9	v	ROVERS	29

A. Keegan		I. Markham	
A. Macklin		C. Young	
J. Maloney	*3 Goals*	J. Moore	*(D. Wainwright)*
R. Gemmell		A. Burwell	*3 Tries*
H. Firth		M. Stephenson	*2 Tries*
B. Hancock		R. Millward	*7 Goals*
C. Davidson		C. Cooper	
M. Harrison		T. Clawson	
A. McGlone	*(sent off)*	P. Flanagan	
E. Broom		B. Mennell	
J. Edson	*1 Try*	J. Hickson	
J. Neale	*(sent off)*	P. Lowe	
J. Brown		P. Small	*(G. Young)*

NPS: D. Doyle-Davidson – S. O'Brien

Halftime: 7-10   Ref: R. Jackson (Halifax)   Att: 12,000 (£2,884)

30th July 1969 — Eva Hardaker Memorial Trophy

ROVERS	15	v	HULL	48

I. Markham		A. Keegan	*1 Try; 9 Goals*
C. Young		C. Sullivan	*2 Tries*
A. Burwell	*1 Try*	R. Gemmell	*1 Try*
J. Moore		D. Doyle-Davidson	
P. Longstaff		A. Macklin	*1 Try*
R. Millward	*1 Try; 3 Goals*	B. Hancock	*1 Try*
C. Cooper	*(sent off 20min)*	C. Davidson	*1 Try*
T. Clawson		M. Harrison	
P. Flanagan		R. Firth	*1 Try*
R. Maxwell		S. O'Brien	
(G. Wrigglesworth 40min)		*(sent off 20min)*	
T. Major		C. Forster	
P. Lowe		J. Macklin	*2 Tries*
P. Small	*1 Try*	N. Trotter	

NPS: C. Wallis   NPS: K. Huxley – A. McGlone

Halftime: 2-19   Ref: P. Geraghty (York)   Att: 5,.500 (£1,400)

27th December 1969 — N.R.F.L.

HULL	6	v	ROVERS	4

A. Keegan	I. Markham
C. Sullivan	P. Coupland
R. Gemmell	J. Moore
J. Maloney *2 Goals*	G. Wrigglesworth
H. Firth	D. Wainwright
B. Hancock	R. Millward *2 Goals*
C. Davidson	A. Bunting *(R. Gay 43min)*
M. Harrison	L. Foster *(J. Hickson 45min)*
A. McGlone	C. Wallis
J. Macklin *1 Drop Goal*	S. Wiley
T. Kirchin	P. Lowe
D. Robson	G. Young
J. Brown	P. Small
NPS: A. Macklin – E. Broom	

Halftime: 4-2   Ref: T. Keane (Oldham)   Att: 13,000 (£3,000)

14th August 1970 — Eva Hardaker Memorial Trophy

HULL	12	v	ROVERS	12

A. Keegan	I. Markham *1 Try*
H. Firth *1 Try*	M. Stephenson
C. Sullivan *1 Try*	R. Norrie
N. Oliver	M. Rooms *(R. Gay)*
A. Macklin	D. Wainwright
B. Hancock	R. Millward *3 Goals*
C. Davidson *2 Goals*	C. Cooper
M. Harrison	S. Wiley
A. McGlone	P. Flanagan
C. Forster	B. Mennell
T. Kirchin	P. Lowe *1 Try (J. Hickson)*
K. Boxall	G. Young
J. Brown *1 Drop Goal*	C. Wallis
NPS: P. Ibbertson	

Halftime: 5-5   Ref: W.H. Thompson (Huddersfield)   Att: 5,000

27th March 1970 — N.R.F.L.

ROVERS	10	v	HULL	10

I. Markham	A. Keegan
M. Stephenson	C. Sullivan *1 Try*
P. Longstaff	R. Gemmell
G. Wrigglesworth	J. Maloney *2 Goals*
P. Coupland *1 Try*	H. Firth
R. Millward *1 Try; 1 Goal*	K. Huxley
C. Cooper	C. Davidson
T. Clawson *1 Goal*	M. Harrison
P. Flanagan	A. McGlone
S. Wiley	C. Forster
P. Lowe	T. Kirchin *1 Try*
G. Young	E. Broom
C. Wallis	P. Ibbertson
NPS: B. Brook – P. Rose	*NPS: A. Macklin – K. Boxall*

Halftime: 2-5   Ref: S. Shepherd (Oldham)   Att: 8,540 (£1,802)

28th August 1970 — Yorkshire Cup (1st Round)

ROVERS	9	v	HULL	27

I. Markham *(M. Rooms)*	M. Owbridge
M. Stephenson	H. Firth *1 Try*
J. Moore	C. Sullivan *3 Tries (A. Geraghty)*
R. Willett *1 Try*	K. Huxley
P. Coupland	A. Macklin
R. Millward	B. Hancock
C. Cooper	C. Davidson
T. Clawson *3 Goals*	M. Harrison
P. Flanagan	A. McGlone
S. Wiley	C. Forster
G. Young *(E. Palmer)*	T. Kirchin
P. Rose	K. Boxall *6 Goals*
C. Wallis	P. Ibbertson *1 Try*
	NPS: N. Trotter

Halftime: 4-18   Ref: T. Keane (Oldham)   Att: 7,337 (£1,957)

3rd November 1970 — BBC2 Floodlit Trophy
(2nd Round)

ROVERS	18	v	HULL	8

P. Coupland	M. Owbridge
M. Stephenson	H. Firth
J. Moore *1 Try*	C. Sullivan *1 Try*
R. Willett	T. Devonshire
M. Rooms *1 Try*	A. Macklin
B. Brook	B. Hancock
C. Cooper *(sent off 33min)*	C. Davidson *(sent off 60min)*
T. Clawson *5 Goals*	M. Harrison
P. Flanagan *1 Drop Goal*	A. McGlone *1 Try*
(sent off 54min)	
C. Wallis	E. Broom *1 Goal*
P. Lowe	T. Kirchin
P. Rose	K. Boxall
G. Young	N. Trotter
NPS: I. Markham – S. Wiley	*NPS: K. Huxley – P. Ibbertson*

Halftime: 8-0   Ref: D.S. Brown (Dewsbury)   Att: 4,540

9th April 1971 — N.R.F.L.

HULL	26	v	ROVERS	12

M. Owbridge	P. Coupland
C. Sullivan *1 Try*	D. Wainwright
A. Keegan	J. Moore *1 Try*
(T. Devonshire 79min)	
J. Maloney *7 Goals*	I. Markham *1 Try*
A. Macklin *1 Try*	P. Longstaff
B. Hancock *1 Try*	B. Brook
K. Foulkes	P. Daley
M. Harrison	T. Clawson *3 Goals*
A. McGlone	P. Flanagan
C. Forster	C. Sykes *(P. Rose)*
T. Kirchin *1 Try*	C. Wallis
K. Boxall *(E. Broom 79min)*	E. Palmer
N. Trotter	J. Brown
	NPS: G. Druery

Halftime: 9-5   Ref: H. Hunt (Prestbury)   Att: 6,000

26th December 1970 — N.R.F.L.

ROVERS	4	v	HULL	18

P. Coupland	M. Owbridge
K. Downing	C. Sullivan *1 Try*
D. Wainwright	M. Crane
I. Markham	J. Maloney *5 Goals*
M. Rooms	A. Macklin
J. Moore	B. Hancock
P. Daley	C. Davidson *1 Goal*
L. Tonks *(P. Rose 40min)*	M. Harrison
A. Crosby	A. McGlone
T. Clawson *2 Goals*	S. O'Brien *1 Try*
P. Lowe	T. Kirchin
G. Young	D. Robson
C. Wallis	P. Ibbertson
NPS: B. Brook	*NPS: D. Doyle-Davidson –*
	E. Broom

Halftime: 0-4   Ref: G. Wilson (Dewsbury)   Att: 5,633 (£1,088)

23rd July 1971 — Eva Hardaker Memorial Trophy

ROVERS	20	v	HULL	8

I. Markham	M. Owbridge
M. Stephenson	C. Sullivan *1 Try*
P. Coupland *1 Try*	T. Devonshire
G. Kirkpatrick	J. Maloney *1 Goal*
P. Longstaff	A. Macklin
R. Millward	B. Hancock
P. Daley *2 Tries (C. Cooper)*	K. Foulkes *1 Try*
T. Clawson *4 Goals*	M. Harrison
P. Flanagan	A. McGlone *(R. Firth)*
S. Wiley	E. Broom *(J. Harrison)*
C. Wallis	T. Kirchin
P. Rose *(E. Palmer)*	K. Boxall
J. Brown *1 Try*	P. Ibbertson

Halftime: 9-3   Ref: H. Cook (Beverley)   Att: 4,500 (£1,349)

April 1984. Hull's Dave Topliss gets away from the Rovers' cover. Photo by courtesy of Eddie Rolmanis.

Paul Rose. Photo by courtesy of Hull Daily Mail.

Mike Smith, Hull K.R. Photo by courtesy of Hull Daily Mail.

Tracy Lazenby. Photo by courtesy of Hull Daily Mail.

Steve Crooks. Photo by courtesy of Hull Daily Mail.

27th December 1971 — N.R.F.L.

HULL	20	v	ROVERS	3

M. Kendle *1 Try; 2 Goals*	I. Markham
C. Sullivan *1 Try*	M. Stephenson
T. Devonshire	P. Coupland *1 Try*
M. Crane	P. Longstaff
H. Firth *1 Try*	D. Wainwright
B. Hancock	S. Hartley *(P. Daley)*
D. Doyle-Davidson	T. Hudson
M. Harrison	N. Dawson *(J. Hickson)*
A. Duke	P. Flanagan
J. Harrison *1 Try*	J. Millington
T. Kirchin	P. Lowe
K. Boxall *2 Goals (D. Robson)*	E. Palmer
N. Trotter	G. Young
NPS: A. Macklin	

Halftime: 13-3   Ref: G. Kershaw (York)   Att: 6,300 (£1,700)

3rd February 1972 — R.L. Cup (1st Round)

HULL	7	v	ROVERS	5

M. Kendle	I. Markham
C. Sullivan	M. Stephenson *1 Try*
T. Devonshire	P. Coupland
M. Crane	G. Kirkpatrick
H. Firth	G. Dunn
B. Hancock *1 Try*	R. Millward *1 Goal*
K. Foulkes	T. Hudson
M. Harrison	N. Dawson *(J. Hickson)*
A. Duke	P. Flanagan
J. Harrison	J. Millington
T. Kirchin	P. Lowe
J. Boxall *2 Goals*	J. Neale
N. Trotter	J. Brown
NPS: D. Doyle-Davidson –	*NPS: J. Moore*
P. Ibbertson	

Halftime: 5-0   Ref: T. Keane (Oldham)   Att: 7,100

31st March 1972 — N.R.F.L.

ROVERS	9	v	HULL	10

I. Markham	M. Kendle *2 Goals; 2 Drop Goals*
P. Longstaff	C. Sullivan
P. Coupland *1 Goal*	T. Devonshire
G. Kirkpatrick	R. Cowan
G. Dunn	A. Macklin
J. Moore *1 Try*	B. Hancock
P. Daley	C. Davidson
N. Dawson *2 Goals*	K. Boxall
(E. Palmer 60min)	
D. Heslop	A. McGlone *1 Drop Goal*
J. Neale	H. Aston
R. Cardy	T. Kirchin
J. Hickson	M. Crane
P. Lowe	N. Trotter
NPS: S. Hartley	*NPS: S. Portz – D. Jervis*

Halftime: 2-8   Ref: M. Naughton (Widnes)   Att: 6,123

12th August 1972 — Eva Hardaker Memorial Trophy

HULL	43	v	ROVERS	8

M. Owbridge	I. Markham
C. Sullivan *2 Tries*	S. Leighton
K. Huxley *1 Try*	P. Longstaff
S. Portz	G. Kirkpatrick *1 Try*
H. Firth *1 Try*	D. Hall *1 Goal*
B. Hancock *1 Try*	S. Hartley
K. Foulkes	T. Hudson
M. Harrison	D. Windmill
A. Duke	P. Flanagan
A. McGlone	J. Neale
K. Boxall *1 Try; 4 Goals*	P. Rose
M. Crane *1 Try*	P. Lowe
P. Ibbertson *2 Tries*	J. Brown
Subs: A. Macklin	*Subs: P. Daley*
J. Harrison	*J. Millington*
L. Casey	*J. Moore*
M. Kendle: 4 Goals	*Hutchinson: 1 Try*

Halftime: 12-2   Ref: F. Lindop (Wakefield)   Att: 2,800

26th December 1972 — N.R.F.L.

ROVERS	15	v	HULL	11

R. Smithies *2 Tries*	M. Owbridge
M. Stephenson	R. Shaw *1 Try*
G. Dunn	S. Portz *1 Try*
P. Coupland *3 Goals*	J. Maloney *1 Goal*
D. Hick	A. Macklin *1 Try*
S. Hartley	A. Geraghty
T. Hudson	G. Williams *(K. Foulkes)*
D. Windmill *1 Try*	K. Boxall
P. Flanagan	R. Firth
E. Barnard	M. Walker
P. Lowe	L. Casey
J. Hickson *(N. Dawson)*	M. Crane *(A. Drew)*
J. Moore	N. Trotter
NPS: P. Daley	

Halftime: 10-3   Ref: W.H. Thompson (Huddersfield)   Att: 4,228 (£1,125)

12th August 1973 — Eva Hardaker Memorial Trophy

ROVERS	13	v	HULL	19

G. Kirkpatrick	A. Geraghty
R. Woodhead *2 Goals*	C. Sullivan *2 Tries*
G. Dunn *2 Tries*	T. Devonshire
S. Leighton	J. Maloney *5 Goals*
D. Hick	A. Macklin *(A. Salmon)*
S. Hartley	B. Hancock
S. Pinkney	K. Foulkes
D. Windmill	M. Harrison
P. Flanagan	K. Boxall *(L. Casey)*
J. Millington *(N. Dawson)*	A. Wardell
R. Holdstock	N. Trotter *1 Try*
S. Wiley *(P. Lowe 1 Try)*	D. Robson
P. Rose *(D. Heslop)*	C. Cooper
	NPS: R. Edmonds – K. Tindall

Halftime: 0-14   Ref: T. Keane (Oldham)   Att: 2,316 (£776)

20th April 1973 — N.R.F.L.

HULL	17	v	ROVERS	13

K. Huxley	P. Coupland
C. Sullivan	M. Rooms *(M. Stephenson)*
C. Davidson *(A. Marshall)*	G. Dunn *2 Tries*
S. Portz *(C. Cooper 1 Goal)*	P. Longstaff
A. Macklin *1 Try*	G. Kirkpatrick *1 Try*
T. Devonshire *1 Goal*	R. Millward *2 Goals*
K. Foulkes	T. Hudson
M. Harrison	N. Dawson *(R. Holdstock)*
K. Boxall *5 Goals*	P. Flanagan
D. Robson	D. Windmill
K. Tindall	J. Neale
A. Wardell	J. Millington
L. Casey	P. Lowe

Halftime: 4-5   Ref: E. Lawrenson (Warrington)   Att: 6,300 (£1,700)

3rd February 1974 — R.L. Cup (1st Round)

HULL	2	v	ROVERS	13

A. Geraghty	P. Coupland
C. Sullivan	S. Leighton
M. Crane	G. Dunn
B. Hancock	D. Hall *1 Goal*
A. Gibbons	D. Hick
T. Devonshire	M. Stephenson *1 Try*
C. Davidson *1 Goal (I. Stenton)*	T. Hudson *1 Goal*
M. Harrison	J. Millington *1 Try (sent off 77 min)*
A. McGlone	P. Flanagan
M. Hicks	P. Rose
A. Salmon	A. Fitzgibbon
B. Kear *(A. Wardell-sent off 77min)*	S. Wiley
L. Casey	J. Moore *1 Try*
	NPS: S. Nuttall – I. Madley

Halftime: 2-11   Ref: S. Shepherd (Oldham)   Att: 8,800

18th August 1974 — Eva Hardaker Memorial Trophy

HULL	13	v	ROVERS	24

A. Geraghty *(A. Salmon)*	R. Smithies
A. Macklin	S. Pinkney
S. Portz *1 Try*	D. Hall *2 Tries*
I. Stenton	N. Fox *6 Goals*
T. Devonshire *1 Try*	G. Dunn *(sent off)*
B. Hancock	B. Watson *1 Try*
C. Davidson *1 Try; 2 Goals*	T. Hudson
S. O'Brien *(A. Wardell-sent off)*	T. Ramshaw
A. Duke *(A. McGlone)*	P. Flanagan *(I. Madley 1 Try)*
J. Macklin	J. Millington
K. Tindall *(B. Kear)*	R. Holdstock *(G. Kirkpatrick)*
D. Robson	C. Wallis *(J. Moore)*
L. Casey	J. Brown

Halftime: 3-10   Ref: F. Lindop (Wakefield)   Att: 2,400

1st January 1975 — Division Two

HULL	10	v	ROVERS	10

S. Portz	R. Smithies
A. Macklin	G. Dunn *1 Try*
M. Crane *1 Try*	D. Hall
B. Hancock	B. Watson *(P. Coupland)*
H. Firth	C. Sullivan *1 Try*
S. Lane *1 Try*	S. Hartley
K. Foulkes	R. Millward *2 Goals*
A. Banham *(A. Salmon)*	J. Millington
A. Duke	I. Madley *(J. Moore)*
A. Wardell	S. Lyons
K. Boxall	P. Rose
L. Casey	C. Wallis
C. Davidson *2 Goals*	J. Brown
NPS: B. Waltham	

Halftime: 0-10   Ref: W.H. Thompson (Huddersfield)   Att: 7,052

26th December 1974 — Division Two

ROVERS	19	v	HULL	12

R. Smithies	A. Geraghty *(S. Portz)*
G. Dunn	A. Macklin
D. Hall *1 Try*	M. Crane
B. Watson	B. Hancock
C. Sullivan	H. Firth *1 Try*
S. Hartley	S. Lane
R. Millward	K. Foulkes *(A. Salmon)*
J. Millington	A. Banham *1 Try*
D. Heslop	A. Duke
S. Lyons	A. Wardell
P. Rose *1 Try (J. Moore)*	K. Boxall
N. Fox *1 Try; 5 Goals*	L. Casey
C. Wallis	C. Davidson *3 Goals*
NPS: P. Coupland	

Halftime: 11-9   Ref: F. Lindop (Wakefield)   Att: 6,016 (£1,855)

10th August 1975 — Eva Hardaker Memorial Trophy

ROVERS	28	v	HULL	25

B. Watson *1 Try; 1 Goal*	P. Hunter
G. Kirkpatrick	A. Macklin
A. Burwell *1 Try*	G. Clark *2 Tries*
S. Hartley *1 Try*	M. Crane *1 Try; 1 Goal*
C. Sullivan *1 Try*	S. Portz
G. Turner *1 Try; 1 Goal*	B. Hancock
S. Pinkney	R. Edmonds
J. Millington	A. Banham *1 Try (sent off)*
C. Dickinson	A. Duke
R. Holdstock	B. Kear
J. Cunningham *3 Goals*	K. Tindall
J. Moore	M. Walker
M. Hughes *1 Try*	L. Casey
Subs: S. Leighton	*Subs: S. Lane 1 Try*
I. Robinson	*B. Waltham*
Jones	*K. Boxall 4 Goals*
P. Edmonds	*A. Salmon*

Halftime: 18-8   Ref: D.G. Kershaw (Easingwold)   Att: 2,729 (£1,190)

8th August 1976 — Eva Hardaker Memorial Trophy

HULL	28	v	ROVERS	23

G. Robinson *3 Goals*	D. Wallace	
A. Macklin	G. Dunn *(W. Youngman)*	
G. Clark	I. Robinson *(S. Hartley 2 tries)*	
S. Portz *1 Try*	D. Hall *(S. Leighton)*	
K. Barr	C. Sullivan	
B. Hancock *1 Try*	G. Turner	
K. Foulkes *(C. Davidson)*	T. Lynn *1 Try (D. Hall)*	
M. Hicks *1 Try (K. Tindall)*	N. Lawson	
A. Duke *(I. Crowther)*	D. Heslop	
A. Wardell *(A. Banham)*	P. Edmonds *(E. Holbrook)*	
K. Boxall *2 Tries; 2 Goals*	A. Ackroyd *1 Try; 4 Goals*	
A. Salmon *(M. Crane)*	E. Holbrook *(R. Norrie 1 Try)*	
M. Walker *1 Try*	M. Hughes *(M. Davidson)*	
NPS: B. Waltham		

Halftime: 18-12   Ref: W.H. Thompson (Huddersfield)
Att: 3,214

14th August 1977 — Eva Hardaker Memorial Trophy

ROVERS	29	v	HULL	18

S. Leighton	D. Marshall *3 Goals*
G. Dunn	G. Bray
M. Smith *1 Try*	C. Lazenby
I. Robinson *2 Tries*	A. Salmon
W. Youngman *2 Tries*	A. Macklin
D. Hall *4 Goals*	B. Hancock
A. Agar	K. Foulkes
J. Millington *1 Try*	K. Tindall
D. Heslop	A. Duke
D. Watkinson	K. Boxall *3 Tries*
D. Hossell	J. Crampton
J. Moore	M. Walker
M. Hughes *1 Try*	M. Crane *1 Try*

Subs: D. Wallace	Subs: P. Ibbertson	N. Trotter
S. Nuttall	P. Flanagan	Gibson
A.N. Other	A. Marshall	M. Sutton
I. Madley		

Halftime: 13-0   Ref: R. Moore (Wakefield)   Att: 3,600

26th February 1977 — R.L. Cup (2nd Round)

ROVERS	12	v	HULL	9

C. Tyrer *4 Goals*	D. Marshall *3 Goals*
G. Dunn	G. Bray
M. Smith *(A. Agar)*	G. Clark
B. Watson	B. Hancock *1 Try*
C. Sullivan	A. Macklin
S. Hartley	M. Stephenson
R. Millward *1 Drop Goal*	C. Davidson
J. Millington	K. Tindall
D. Heslop	A. Duke
P. Rose	A. Wardell
P. Lowe *1 Try*	K. Boxall
M. Hughes	J. Crampton *(N. Trotter)*
L. Casey	M. Crane
NPS: D. Watkinson	*NPS: A. Salmon*

Halftime: 4-6   Ref: P. Massey (Salford)   Att: 10,939

2nd October 1977 — Division one

ROVERS	13	v	HULL	20

D. Hall *1 Goal*	P. Hunter
G. Dunn	G. Bray
I. Robinson *1 Goal*	G. Clark *1 Try*
B. Watson	D. Marshall *6 Goals*
C. Sullivan	A. Macklin
S. Hartley *2 Tries*	B. Hancock *1 Drop Goal*
R. Millward	P. Hall
J. Millington	K. Tindall
D. Heslop	A. Duke
J. Cunningham *1 Try*	M. Sutton *(P. Ibbertson)*
P. Lowe	A. Salmon
P. Rose	K. Boxall
M. Hughes	M. Crane *1 Try; 1 Drop Goal*
NPS: A. Agar – R. Holdstock	*NPS: K. Barr*

Halftime: 8-12   Ref: P.Massey (Salford)   Att: 11,041

26th February 1978 — R.L. Cup (1st Round)

HULL	9	v	ROVERS	7

G. Robinson	C. Tyrer *2 Goals (sent off)*
G. Bray	G. Dunn
G. Turner	D. Hall
D. Marshall	B. Watson
A. Macklin *1 Try*	C. Sullivan *1 Try*
B. Hancock	S. Hartley
K. Hepworth *(P. Hall)*	R. Millward
K. Tindall	J. Cunningham
A. Duke	D. Watkinson
V. Farrar	B. Lockwood
K. Boxall *3 Goals*	P. Lowe *(sent off)*
S. Norton	P. Rose
C. Davidson *(M. Sutton)*	L. Casey
	NPS: A. Agar – R. Holdstock

Halftime: 4-5   Ref: R. Campbell (Widnes)   Att: 16,001

24th March 1978 — Division One

HULL	18	v	ROVERS	10

G. Robinson	C. Tyrer *2 Goals*
G. Bray	G. Dunn
K. Barr	D. Hall
G. Turner *1 Try: 2 Goals*	B. Watson
A. Macklin *1 Try*	C. Sullivan
B. Hancock	S. Hartley *(M. Smith)*
T. Lynn	R. Millward *1 Try*
K. Tindall	J. Millington *(R. Holdstock)*
A. Duke *1 Try*	D. Heslop
V. Farrar	B. Lockwood
P. Young	P. Lowe
K. Boxall *1 Try; 1 Goal*	P. Rose *1 Try*
S. Norton *(C. Davidson)*	L. Casey
NPS: I. Wilson	

Halftime: 16-10   Ref: M. Naughton (Widnes)   Att: 11,537

6th August 1978 — Eva Hardaker Memorial Trophy

HULL	28	v	ROVERS	24

A.N. Other *5 Goals*	D. Hall *1 Try: 1 Goal*
G. Bray	G. Dunn *1 Try*
C. Harrison *1 Try*	P. Lowe *1 Try*
K. Barr *1 Try*	I. Robinson *1 Try*
A. Macklin	G. McHugh
I. Wilson *2 Tries*	S. Hartley
C. Davidson	A. Agar *2 Goals*
K. Tindall	J. Cunningham *2 Tries*
I. Crowther *1 Try*	D. Heslop
V. Farrar	D. Watkinson
K. Boxall	B. Lockwood
M. Sutton *1 Try*	Davidson
P. Young	L. Casey
Subs: (All Played)	*Subs: (All Played)*
C. Lazenby	*S. Leighton*
D. Hodgson	*S. Nuttall*
S. Norton	*S. Crooks*
C. Sanderson	*J. Millington*

Halftime: 15-8   Ref: T. Beaumont (Huddersfield)   Att: 4,492

5th August 1979 — Eva Hardaker Memorial Trophy

HULL	27	v	ROVERS	20

I. Wilson	D. Hall *1 Try (W. Youngman)*
A. Macklin *1 Try*	G. Dunn
D. Noble	I Robinson *2 Goals*
C. Harrison *1 Try (G. Robinson)*	B. Watson *(S. Leighton 1 Try)*
P. Prendiville *(S. Dennison)*	S. Hubbard *2 Goals (S. Nuttall)*
J. Newlove	S. Hartley *2 Tries*
C. Pickerill *1 Try (C. Sanderson)*	A. Agar
C. Lazenby *1 Try: 6 Goals*	J. Millington
I. Crowther	D. Heslop
V. Farrar	S. Crooks *(S. Mowforth)*
K. Boxall *1 Try*	G. Clarkson
M. Sutton *(K. Hepworth)*	G. Douglas
G. Peacham *(W. Mallinson)*	Bennett

Halftime: 12-10   Ref: F. Lindop (Wakefield)   Att: 5,005

October 1984. Rovers' "Zook" Ema tries to get away from Steve Norton's tackle. Photo by courtesy of Eddie Rolmanis.

Hull's Lee Crooks unloads the ball before Mark Broadhurst (left) can tackle him. October 1986. Photo by courtesy of Eddie Rolmanis.

7th October 1979 — Division One

HULL	20	v	ROVERS	20

G. Robinson	S. Leighton
G. Bray *1 Try*	S. Hubbard *1 Try: 4 Goals*
C. Harrison	M. Smith
G. Evans *(G. Walters 1 Try)*	B. Watson
P. Prendiville *1 Try: 1 Goal*	C. Sullivan *1 Try*
J. Newlove	R. Millward *(S. Hartley)*
C. Pickerill	A. Agar *1 Try*
K. Tindall	R. Holdstock
R. Wileman	D. Heslop
V. Farrar *(K. Boxall 1 Try)*	B. Lockwood
C. Stone	G. Clarkson *(S. Crooks)*
C. Birdsall *3 Goals*	P. Hogan *1 Try*
S. Norton	D. Hall

Halftime: 10-15   Ref: W. Thompson (Huddersfield)   Att: 16,745

4th April 1980 — Division One

ROVERS	29	v	HULL	14

D. Hall	P. Coupland
S. Hubbard *7 Goals*	G. Bray
M. Smith *1 Try*	G. Evans
B. Watson *1 Try*	T. Wilby
C. Sullivan	S. Dennison *3 Goals*
S. Hartley *1 Try*	B. Hancock
P. Harkin	K. Hepworth *2 Tries*
R. Holdstock	C. Lazenby
D. Watkinson	R. Wileman
J. Millington	V. Farrar
P. Hogan *(P. Lowe 1 Try)*	K. Boxall *(G. Lloyd 1 Goal)*
P. Rose	C. Stone
M. Crane *1 Try*	S. Norton
NPS: I. Robinson	*NPS: C. Pickerill*

Halftime: 12-9   Ref: M.Naughton (Widnes)   Att: 15,000

18th December 1979 — BBC2 FLOODLIT TROPHY FINAL

HULL	13	v	ROVERS	3

P. WOODD	I. ROBINSON
G. BRAY	S. HUBBARD *1 Try*
G. EVANS *1 Try*	M. SMITH
P. COUPLAND	B. WATSON
S. DENNISON *1 Try: 2 Goals*	C. SULLIVAN
J. NEWLOVE	D. HALL
K. HEPWORTH	A. AGAR
K. TINDALL	R. HOLDSTOCK
R. WILEMAN	G. TYREMAN
V. FARRAR	B. LOCKWOOD
C. STONE	G. CLARKSON *(S. Hartley)*
K. BOXALL	P. LOWE
(C. BIRDSALL 40min.1 Try)	
S. NORTON	P. HOGAN *(J. MILLINGTON)*
NPS: G. WALTERS	

Halftime: 5-0   Ref: W. Thompson (Huddersfield)

Att: 18,500 (This was a competition record in the last ever Final)

3rd May 1980 — R.L. CUP FINAL (at WEMBLEY)

HULL	5	v	ROVERS	10

P. WOODS	D. HALL
G. BRAY	S. HUBBARD *1 Try; 3 Goals*
G. WALTERS	M. SMITH
T. WILBY *1 Try*	S. HARTLEY
P. PRENDIVILLE	C. SULLIVAN
J. NEWLOVE	R. MILLWARD *1 Drop Goal*
C. PICKERILL	A. AGAR
K. TINDALL	R. HOLDSTOCK
R. WILEMAN	D. WATKINSON
C. STONE	B. LOCKWOOD
C. BIRDSALL	P. LOWE
G. LLOYD *1 Goal*	P. ROSE
S. NORTON	L. CASEY
Subs: B. HANCOCK for J. NEWLOVE	*Subs: P. HOGAN for S. HUBBARD*
V. FARRAR for C. STONE	*J. MILLINGTON for P. ROSE*

Halftime: 3-8   Ref: G.F. Lindop (Wakefield)
Att: 95,000 (£448,202)
Lance Todd Trophy Winner:- B. Lockwood (Rovers)

28th September 1980 — Division One

ROVERS	25	v	HULL	10

I. Robinson (G. McHugh)	G. Robinson
S. Hubbard 1 Try; 1 Goal	S. Dennison
M. Smith 1 Try	G. Walters (sent off 62min)
P. Hogan 1 Try; 2 Goals	T. Wilby
W. Youngman 2 Tries	P. Prendiville
S. Hartley 1 Try	I. Wilson
P. Harkin 1 Drop Goal	C. Pickerill
S. Crooks	K. Tindall
R. Price	I. Crowther
D. Watkinson (sent off 62min)	C. Stone (C. Harrison 64min)
P. Lowe	C. Birdsall 1 Try
C. Dixon (G. Douglas)	G. Lloyd 2 Goals
L. Casey	S. Norton 1 Try
	NPS: V. Farrar

Halftime: 16-0   Ref: R. Campbell (Widnes)

Att: 13,681 (£10,700)

16th May 1981 — PREMIERSHIP FINAL (at HEADINGLEY

HULL	7	v	ROVERS	11

P. WOODS 2 Goals	P. PROCTOR
G. PEACHAM	S. HUBBARDS 1 Goal
D. ELLIOTT	M. SMITH 1 Try
T. WILBY	P. HOGAN 1 Try
P. PRENDIVILLE	P. MUSCROFT
B. BANKS	S. HARTLEY 1 Try
A. DEAN	P. HARKIN
K. TINDALL	R. HOLDSTOCK
R. WILEMAN	D. WATKINSON
C. STONE	J. MILLINGTON
T. SKERRETT	P. LOWE
(sub: I. MADLEY 70min)	
M. CRANE 1 Try	L. CASEY
S. NORTON	D. HALL (sub: C. BURTON)
NPS: R. CHESTER	NPS: K. WATSON

Halftime: 2-8   Ref: J. Holdsworth (Leeds)   Att: 30,000

17th April 1981 — Division One

HULL	16	v	ROVERS	17

P.Woods 5 Goals	I. Robinson
G. Bray	S. Hubbard 1 Try; 1 Goal
G. Walters 1 Try	M. Smith
T. Wilby	P. Hogan 1 Try
P. Prendiville	P. Muscroft
B. Banks	S. Hartley 1 Try
A. Dean 1 Try	S. Sanderson
K. Tindall	J. Millington
R. Wileman	R. Price
T. Skerrett	S. Crooks
M. Crane	P. Lowe 2 Tries
C. Birdsall (I. Madley)	C. Burton
S. Norton	D. Hall (P. Proctor)
NPS: C. Pickerill	NPS: C. Dixon

Halftime: 9-9   Ref: F. Lindop (Wakefield)   Att: 18,500

Record for Division One

3rd January 1982 — Division One

HULL	11	v	ROVERS	1

G. Kemble	G. Fairburn 1 Drop Goal
D. O'Hara	S. Hubbard
C. Harrison	M. Smith
J. Leuluai 1 Try	P. Proctor
P. Prendiville 1 Try	P. Muscroft
T. Day	S. Hartley
K. Harkin	P. Harkin
T. Skerrett	R. Holdstock
R. Wileman	D. Watkinson
(G. Lloyd 40min 1 Try; 1 Goal)	
C. Stone	J. Millington (P. Lowe 40min)
M. Crane	C. Burton (S. Crooks 60min)
L. Crooks (K. Tindall 70min)	L. Casey
S. Norton	D. Hall

Halftime: 3-1   Ref: G.F. Lindop (Wakefield)   Att: 17,229

23rd January 1982
JOHN PLAYER TROPHY FINAL (at HEADINGLEY)

HULL	12	v	ROVERS	4

B. BANKS	G. FAIRBAIRN *2 Goals*
D. O'HARA	S. HUBBARD
C. HARRISON	M. SMITH
J. LEULUAI	P. HOGAN
P. PRENDIVILLE	P. MUSCROFT
T. DAY	S. HARTLEY
A. DEAN *1 Drop Goal*	P. HARKIN *(C. BURTON 30min)*
(K. HARKIN 53min)	
T. SKERRETT	R. HOLDSTOCK *(sent off 75min)*
R. WILEMAN *1 Try*	D. WATKINSON
C. STONE *(sent off 75min)*	S. CROOKS
M. CRANE	P. LOWE
L. CROOKS *4 Goals*	L. CASEY
S. NORTON	D. HALL
NPS: G. LLOYD	*Sub: J. MILLINGTON for*
	R. HOLDSTOCK (40min)
	HOLDSTOCK for S. CROOKS 70min

Halftime: 5-2   Ref: G.F. Lindop (Wakefield)   Att: 25,245 (£42,987)

22nd September 1982 — Division One

ROVERS	16	v	HULL	12

G. Fairbairn *4 Goals; 2 Drop Goals*	B. Banks
G. Clark	I. Scruton
M. Smith *2 Tries*	S. Evans *1 Try*
P. Hogan	J. Leuluai
S. Hubbard	P. Prendiville
S. Hartley	D. Topliss
J. Walsh	K. Harkin *(A. Dean 74min)*
R. Holdstock	P. Rose *(W. Proctor 44min)*
D. Watkinson	A. Duke
S. Crooks	C. Stone
P. Lowe	S. Norton *1 Try*
L. Casey	L. Crooks *3 Goals*
G. Prohm	M. Crane
NPS: I. Robinson – C. Burton	

Halftime: 4-12   Ref: G. Kershaw (Easingwold)   Att: 13,610

31st March 1982 — Division One

ROVERS	19	v	HULL	13

G. Fairburn *1 Try; 3 Goals*	G. Kemble
S. Hubbard *1 Try*	D. O'Hara
P. Hogan *1 Try*	T. Day
I. Robinson	S. Evans
P. Muscroft	P. Prendiville
M. Smith	D.Topliss *1 Try*
J. Walsh	K. Harkin
J. Millington *(P. Edmonds)*	K. Tindall *(D. Busfield)*
D. Watkinson *1 Drop Goal*	A. Duke
S. Crooks	T. Skerrett
K. Watson	M. Crane
C. Burton *1 Try*	G. Lloyd *5 Goals*
D. Hall	S. Norton
NPS: D. Laws	*NPS: C. Harrison*

Halftime: 14-2   Ref: J. Holdsworth (Leeds)
Att: 15,574 (£13,500)

8th April 1983 — Division One

HULL	21	v	ROVERS	3

G. Kemble *1 Try (sent off 55min)*	J. Lydiat *(sent off 55min)*
D. O'Hara *1 Try*	D. Laws
T. Day	I. Robinson
J. Leuluai *1 Try*	G. Fairbairn (S. Hartley)
P. Prendiville *1 Try; 3 Goals*	G. Prohm
D. Topliss	M. Smith
K. Harkin	G. Smith
P. Edmonds *(M. Crane 29min 1 Try)*	J. Millington
K. Bridges	D. Watkinson
C. Stone *(B. Banks 58min)*	R. Holdstock
P. Rose	A. Kelly
T. Skerrett	P. Hogan
S. Norton	T. Lazenby *(D. Hall 40min 1 Try)*

Halftime: 10-0   Ref:W.H. Thompson (Huddersfield)
Att: 20,596
(New 1st Division Record)

2nd October 1983 — Division One

HULL	**8**	v	**ROVERS**	**23**

J. Leuluai	G. Fairbairn *3 Goals*
P. Solal *(G. Schofield 53 min)*	G. Clark *2 Tries*
S. Evans	M. Smith *1 Try*
B. Banks	G. Prohm
P. Prendiville *2 Goals*	D. Laws *1 Try*
F. Ah Kuoi	S. Hartley
K. Harkin	G. Smith *1 Drop Goal*
T. Skerrett	R. Holdstock
S. Patrick	D. Watkinson
C. Stone	L. Casey
P. Rose *(W. Proctor 53min)*	M. Broadhurst
L. Crooks *1 Try*	P. Hogan
M. Crane	D. Hall *(T. Lazenby 74min)*
	NPS: P. Harkin

Halftime: 2-8   Ref: W. Thompson (Huddersfield)   Att: 18,185

20th April 1984 — Division One

ROVERS	**16**	v	**HULL**	**36**

G. Fairbairn	G. Kemble
G. Clark *1 Try*	S. Evans
M. Smith	G. Schofield *8 Goals*
G. Prohm	J. Leuluai *1 Try*
S. Hartley *(J. Lydiat 66min)*	D. O'Hara
J. Dorahy *1 Try; 2 Goals*	D. Topliss *1 Try*
G. Smith *1 Try (J. Millington 30min)*	F. Ah Kuoi *2 Tries*
M. Broadhurst	P. Edmonds
C. Rudd	N. Puckering
	(L. Crooks 55min 1 Try)
L. Casey *(sent off 46min)*	P. Rose *(A. Dannatt 66min)*
C. Burton	W. Proctor
P. Hogan	S. Norton
D. Hall	G. Divorty

Halftime: 10-8   Ref: R. Campbell (Widnes)   Att: 16,084

7th October 1984 — Division One

ROVERS	**26**	v	**HULL**	**17**

J. Lydiat *5 Goals (P. Harkin 54min*	G. Kemble
J. Lydiat 60min)	
G. Clark	K. James
P. Hogan	G. Schofield *4 Goals*
G. Prohm *1 Try*	S. Evans *1 Try*
D. Laws *1 Try*	D. O'Hara *1 Try*
S. Hartley	F. Ah Kuoi *1 Drop Goal*
G. Smith	A. Collinson *(D. Topliss 50min)*
M. Broadhurst	P. Edmonds *(P. Rose 62min)*
D. Watkinson	S. Patrick
A. Ema	L. Crooks
C. Burton	A. Dannatt
A. Kelly *1 Try*	W. Proctor
M. Smith *1 Try*	S. Norton
NPS: C. Rudd	

Halftime: 2-16   Ref: J. Holdsworth (Leeds)   Att: 14,481

27th October 1984 — YORKSHIRE CUP FINAL
(at BOOTHFERRY PARK, HULL)

HULL	**29**	v	**ROVERS**	**12**

G. KEMBLE *2 Tries*	G. FAIRBAIRN *1 Try*
J. LEULUAI	G. CLARK
G. SCHOFIELD	
4 Goals; 1 Drop Goal	I. ROBINSON *1 Try*
S.EVANSA *1 Try*	G. PROHM
D. O'HARA	D. LAWS
F. AH KUOI	M. SMITH
P. STERLING	P. HARKIN *(C. RUDD 74min)*
P. EDMONDS	M. BROADHURST
S. PATRICK	D. WATKINSON
L. CROOKS *1 Try*	A. EMA *(S. HARTLEY 51min)*
S. NORTON *1 Try*	C. BURTON
W. PROCTOR	A. KELLY
G. DIVORTY	D. HALL *1 Try*
(P. ROSE 70min sent off 71min)	
NPS: D. TOPLISS	

Halftime: 8-12   Ref: F. Lindop (Wakefield)   Att: 25,243 (£68,639)

26th January 1985 — JOHN PLAYER TROPHY FINAL
(at BOOTHFERRY PARK, HULL)

HULL	0	v	ROVERS	12

G. KEMBLE	G. FAIRBAIRN
(G. SCHOFIELD 21min)	
S. EVANS	G. CLARK *1 Try*
F. AH KUOI	I. ROBINSON
J. LEULUAI	G. PROHM *1 Try*
D. O'HARA	D. LAWS
D. TOPLISS	M. SMITH
P. STERLING	P. HARKIN
P. EDMONDS	M. BROADHURST
(A. DANNATT 63min)	
S. PATRICK	D. WATKINSON
P. ROSE	A. EMA
L. CROOKS	C. BURTON
W. PROCTOR	P. HOGAN *1 Try*
G. DIVORTY	G. MILLER

NPS: J. LYDIAT – L. CASEY

Halftime: 0-8   Ref: S. Wall (Leigh)   Att: 25,326 (£69,555)

15th September 1985 — Yorkshire Cup (1st Round)

ROVERS	12	v	HULL	10

G. Fairbairn	G. Kemble
G. Clark	K. James *(P. Prendiville 72min)*
J. Dorahy *2 Goals*	J. Portz
G. Prohm	J. Leuluai
D. Laws	D. O'Hara *1 Try*
G. Smith	F. Ah Kuoi
P. Harkin *(J. Lydiat 40min)*	A. Gascoigne
Des Harrison *(A. Kelly 54min)*	T. Skerrett
D. Watkinson	S. Patrick
A. Ema	N. Puckering *(C. Arnett 65min)*
P. Hogan *2 Tries*	P. Rose
C. Burton	L. Crooks *1 Try*
G. Miller	G. Divorty *1 Goal*

Halftime: 4-4   Ref: F. Lindop (Wakefield)   Att: 10,116

12th April 1985 — Division One

HULL	12	v	ROVERS	36

J. Leuluai	G. Fairbairn *6 Goals*
P. Prendiville	J. Lydiat
G. Schofield *1 Goal*	I. Robinson *(B. Miller 22min)*
S. Evans *(A. Dannatt 25min)*	G. Prohm *1 Try*
D. O'Hara	D. Laws
D. Topliss	M. Smith *2 Tries*
J. Portz	G. Smith
P. Edmonds *1 Try*	R. Holdstock *1 Try*
L. Crooks *1 Goal*	D. Watkinson
P. Rose	A. Ema
W. Proctor *(C. Arnett 36min)*	M. Broadhurst
A. Dannatt *(J. Muggleton 22min 1 Try)*	D. Hall *1 Try*
G. Divorty	G. Miller *1 Try (P. Harkin 57min)*

Halftime: 6-12   Ref: R. Whitfield (Widnes)   Att: 13,007

6th October 1985 — Division One

HULL	28	v	ROVERS	6

G. Kemble	J. Lydiat
P. Eastwood	P. Hogan
G. Schofield *2 Tries; 2 Goals*	I. Robinson *1 Try*
J. Leuluai	G. Prohm
D. O'Hara *1 Try*	D. Laws
F. Ah Kuoi	J. Dorahy *1 Goal*
A. Gascoigne *1 Try*	G. Smith
T. Skerrett *(S. Vass 76min 1 Try)*	Des Harrison *(P. Johnston 40min)*
S. Patrick	D. Watkinson
N. Puckering	A. Ema
G. Gerard	C. Burton
L. Crooks *2 Goals (G. Divorty 65min)*	A. Kelly
S. Norton	G. Miller

NPS: C. Rudd

Halftime: 12-2   Ref: K. Allatt (Southport)   Att: 13,041

New Zealander, Gordon Smith, scores the first try between Rovers and Hull, October 1986 at Craven Park, watched by Fred Ah Kuoi. Rovers won 29-6 before a crowd of 7,980. Photo by courtesy of Hull Daily Mail.

8th February 1986 — R.L. Cup (1st Round)

ROVERS	22	v	HULL	6

G. Fairbairn	G. Kemble
G. Clark	P. Eastwood
M. Smith *1 Try*	G. Schofield
G. Prohm	J. Leuluai
D. Laws	D. O'Hara *1 Try*
J. Dorahy *5 Goals*	S. Evans
P. Harkin	F. Ah Kuoi *(G. Divorty 9min)*
P. Johnston	T. Skerrett *(N. Puckering 40min)*
D. Watkinson	W. Mallinson
A. Ema	G. Gerard
Des Harrison *(A. Kelly 27min 1 Try)*	W. Proctor
P. Hogan *(G. Smith 70min)*	L. Crooks *1 Goal*
G. Miller *1 Try*	S. Norton

Halftime: 8-0   Ref: R. Whitfield (Widnes)   Att: 8,746

5th October 1986 — Division One

ROVERS	29	v	HULL	6

J. Lydiat	S. Hick *(D. Brown 65min)*
G. Clark	M. Brand
J. Dorahy *1 Try; 6 Goals*	G. Schofield *1 Try*
K. Boustead *(R. Stead 42min)*	D. O'Hara
D. Laws	P. McCoid
M. Smith *1 Drop Goal*	F. Ah Kuoi
W. Parker *1 Try*	K. Dick
M. Broadhurst	D. Brown *(J. Sharp 29min)*
D. Watkinson	S. Patrick
A. Ema	S. Crooks *(G. Divorty 60min)*
A. Kelly *1 Try*	A. Dannatt
Des Harrison	L. Crooks *1 Goal*
G. Smith *1 Try (C. Rudd 25min)*	S. Norton

Halftime: 17-0   Ref: D. Fox (Wakefield)   Att: 8,020

22nd April 1986 — Division One

ROVERS	2	v	HULL	28

M. Fletcher *1 Goal*	G. Kemble
R. Stead	M. Brand *1 Try*
G. Sims	G. Schofield *1 Try; 2 Goals*
R. Noble	J. Leuluai *1 Try*
	(F. Ah Kuoi 35 min 1 Try)
S. Smith	D. O'Hara
W. Parker	S. Evans *(J. Leuluai 48min)*
S. Farr *(C. Hutchinson 59min)*	P. Windley
L. Johnston	P. Edmonds
A. Sissons	W. Mallinson
M. Beall *(F. Parker 59min)*	A. Tomlinson *1 Try*
S. Olsen	C. Arnett
C. Harrison	S. Norton *(W. Proctor 69min)*
P. Speckman	G. Divorty *1 Try*

Halftime: 0-4   Ref: R. Campbell (Widnes)   Att: 5,685

17th April 1987 — Division One

HULL	8	v	ROVERS	21

G. Kemble	G. Fairbairn *4 Goals*
P. Eastwood	G. Clark *1 Try*
G. Schofield	A. Thompson
D. O'Hara	K. Boustead *1 Try*
P. McCoid	R. Stead
F. Ah Kuoi	M. Smith
K. Dick *1 Try; 1 Goal*	W. Parker *1 Try; 1 Drop Goal*
A. Dannatt *(L. Crooks 66min)*	Des Harrison
S. Patrick	C. Rudd
S. Crooks	M. Beall
N. Elgar	P. Speckman
L. Crooks *1 Goal*	A. Kelly
(T. Lazenby 60min; W. Proctor 76min)	
S. Norton	G. Smith

NPS: G. Sims – A. Needler

Halftime: 0-2   Ref: R. Whitfield (Widnes)   Att: 9,216

3rd January 1988 — Division One

HULL	2	v	ROVERS	11

P. Fletcher	G. Fairbairn
P. Eastwood	G. Clark *1 Try*
S. Vass	M. Fletcher *3 Goals*
J. Leuluai	P. Mortimer
D. O'Hara	S. Smith *(J. Lydiat 61min)*
G. Pearce *1 Goal*	M. Smith
P. McCaffery	W. Parker *1 Drop Goal*
M. Sutton *(J. Carroll 3min)*	R. Taylor
L. Jackson	D. Watkinson
P. Welham *(N. Puckering 40min)*	A. Ema
D. Brooks	C. Burton
T. Regan	G. Ryan
G. Divorty	G. Smith *(M. Beall 61min)*

Halftime: 2-5   Ref: D.G. Kershaw (Easingwold)   Att: 8,997

2nd January 1989 — Division One

ROVERS	12	v	HULL	15

G. Fairbairn *2 Goals*	P. Fletcher
D. Laws	P. Eastwood
J. Lydiat *(A. Ema 62min)*	D. Moon *1 Try*
J. Irvine	R. Price *(B. Blacker 78min)*
R. Pratt	D. O'Hara
M. Smith	G. Pearce *3 Goals; 1 Drop Goal*
D. Bishop	C. Coleman *1 Try*
M. Porter	S. Crooks *(P. Welham 58min)*
Dave Harrison *1 Try*	L. Jackson
M. Beall	D. Boyle
Des Harrison *(C. Burton 52min)*	T. Wilby
C. Close *1 Try*	J. Sharp
G. Miller	G. Divorty

Halftime: 10.12   Ref: R. Tennant (Castleford)   Att: 8,837

1st April 1988 — Division One

ROVERS	14	v	HULL	21

G. Fairbairn *(J. Lydiat 51min)*	P. Fletcher
G. Clark	P. Eastwood *1 Try*
M. Fletcher *3 Goals* *(G. Fairbairn 73min)*	H. M'Barki
D. Laws	L. Leuluai
R. Stead	D. O'Hara
M.Smith *1 Try* *Goals*	G. Pearce *1 Try; 3 Goals; 3 Drop*
W. Parker *1 Try*	P. McCaffery
M. Beall	S. Crooks
Dave Harrison	S. Patrick *(A. Dannatt 44min)*
A. Ema	J. Carroll *(R. Price 49min)*
C. Burton *(Des Harrison 66min)*	P. Welham *1 Try*
G. Ryan	J. Sharp
G. Smith	G. Divorty

Halftime: 2-17   Ref: F. Lindop (Wakefield)   Att: 7,076

JOINT FIXTURES AGAINST TOURING TEAMS

During the period from 1956 to 1963, the visit to the City of Hull by the Australian or New Zealand Touring Team was marked by a game against a joint Hull/Rovers XIII.

The four matches concerned are as follows:

15th October 1956 (Played at Boothferry Park, Hull)

HULL/ROVERS XIII 14	v	AUSTRALIA	37

T. Buckle *(Rovers)* 4 Goals	Churchill *2 Goals*
K. Gittoes *(Hull)* 1 Try	Moir *2 Tries*
N. Hancock *(Rovers)*	Poole *2 Tries*
B. Coulson *(Rovers)* 1 Try	Payne
B. Shaw *(Rovers)*	Flannery *1 Try*
C. Turner *(Hull)*	Banks
T. Finn *(Hull)*	Connell *1 Try*
M. Scott *(Hull)*	Davies *2 Tries*
T. Harris *(Hull)*	Hammerton
J. Hall *(Rovers)*	Bull *1 Try*
T. Bourton *(Rovers)*	Marsh
H. Markham *(Hull)*	Furner *3 Goals*
W. Drake *(Hull)*	O'Shea

Halftime: 6-11   Ref: M. Coates (Pudsey)   Att: 17,346 (£2,680)

4th October 1961 (Played at The Boulevard)

HULL/ROVERS XIII 17	v	NEW ZEALAND	6

C. Kellett *(Rovers)* 7 Goals	Harrison
A. Mullins *(Rovers)*	Hadfield
T. Major *(Rovers)*	R. Cooke *3 Goals*
T. Hollindrake *(Hull)*	Kennedy
K. Barnwell *(Hull)*	Amer
D. Elliott *(Rovers)*	Bond
A. Bunting *(Rovers)* 1 Try	Farrar
W. Drake *(Hull)*	Butterfield
T. Harris *(Hull)*	Patterson
J. Drake *(Hull)*	Emery
J. Taylor *(Rovers)*	Hammond
H. Poole *(Rovers)*	Tiller
J. Whiteley *(Hull)*	M. Cooke

Halftime: 10-4   Ref: G. Wilson (Dewsbury)   Att: 12,000 (£1,242)

26th October 1959 (Played at Boothferry Park, Hull)

HULL/ROVERS XIII 9	v	AUSTRALIA	29

P. Bateson *(Hull)* 3 Goals	Chapman
G. Matthews *(Hull)*	Parrish *1 Try; 7 Goals*
E. Wilson *(Rovers)*	Boden *1 Try*
G. Garton *(Rovers)*	Wells *1 Try*
R. Moat *(Rovers)*	Irvine
G. Paul *(Rovers)*	Burke *1 Try*
D. Elliott *(Rovers)* 1 Try	Brown *1 Try*
M. Scott *(Hull)*	Rasmussen
T. Harris *(Hull)*	Walsh
J. Drake *(Hull)*	Beattie
D. Holland *(Rovers)*	Purcell
J. Jenkin *(Rovers)*	Mossop
C. Sykes *(Hull)*	Hambly

Halftime: 4-19   Ref: G. Philpott (Leeds)   Att: 15,944 (£2,372)

12th October 1963 (Played at The Boulevard)

HULL/ROVERS XIII 10	v	AUSTRALIA	23

A. Keegan *(Hull)* 2 Goals	Johns *4 Goals*
G. Paul *(Rovers)*	M. Cleary
J. Moore *(Rovers)*	Rushworth *1 Try*
T. Hollindrake *(Hull)* 2 Tries	Lisle
T. Devonshire *(Hull)*	Irvine *2 Tries*
D. Elliott *(Rovers)*	Gleeson
T. Finn *(Hull)*	Stanton *1 Try*
W. Drake *(Hull)*	Ryan *(Sub J. Cleary 25min)*
P. Flanagan *(Rovers)*	Walsh
F. Fox *(Rovers)*	Kelly
E. Bonner *(Rovers)*	Day
L. Chamberlain *(Rovers)*	Wilson
C. Sykes *(Hull)*	Smythe *1 Try*

Halftime: 5-5   Ref: H. Pickersgill (Halifax)   Att: 11,000 (£1,548)

MATCH RECORDS

At the conclusion of the Derby Match at Craven Park on 2nd January 1989, there had been a total of 184 League, Cup and Championship Play-off encounters between the two sides.

Summarised these have been as follows:-

	WINNERS			POINTS SCORED	
	Hull	Rovers	Drawn	Hull	Rovers
League (155 games)	77	68	10	1719	1586
R.L. Cup (11 games)	6	5		102	94
Yorks. Cup (10 Games)	5	5		138	110
J. Player Trophy) (2 Games)	1	1		12	16
BBC2 Trophy (3 Games)	1	2		29	33
Play-Offs (3 Games)	1	2		25	41
TOTAL (184 Games)	91	83	10	2025	1880

At Craven Street:-

Rovers Highest Home Win was 35-4 on 9 April 1909
    "   "   " Defeat was 11-20 On 15 Sept. 1900

At Craven Park:-

Rovers Highest Home win was 39-2 on 4 Oct 1924
    "   "   " Defeat was 16-36 on 20 April 1984

At the Boulevard:-

Hull's Highest Home Win was 33-7 on 26 Dec 1908
    "   "   " Defeat was 12-36 on 12 April 1985

The Highest Scoring Draw between the sides was 20-20 on 7 Oct 1979, at the Boulevard.

HIGHEST ATTENDANCES

Attendances at 'Derby' Matches

Naturally, the highest attendance at a Humberside Derby is the 95,000 which attended Wembley in May 1980 for the never-to-be-forgotten Rugby League Cup Final. The rival supporters gained for themselves the highest praise from the Authorities for their good behaviour after years of appalling violence from Soccer supporters at most of the big occasions. Obviously, the matches within the City of Hull have been restricted in their audience by the size of the grounds. Nowadays, of course, the constraints placed upon the clubs because of safety considerations, have severely limited the crowds which can be accommodated. However, the two sides have played to many large galleries within Hull at the various venues. Insofar as the attendance figures reported are not always completely reliable or accurate, listed below are the highest Derby crowds at the four Hull venues:-

Craven Street: 18,000 (Receipts £1,000)
11th March 1922 — Rugby League Cup (2nd Round)

Craven Park: 22,282 (Receipts £1,300)
7th October 1922 — 1st Derby at Craven Park

Boulevard: 28,000 (Receipts £1,644)
21st April 1923 — Championship Semi-Final

Boothferry Park: 27,670 (Receipts £3,280)
3rd April 1953 — Rovers Home League Match

SUMMARY OF ALL LEAGUE AND CUP GAMES
At THE BOULEVARD

	Games Played:	Hull have won	Rovers have won	Games Drawn	Points Scored Hull	Rovers
League:	77	42	27	8	846	643
R.L. Cup:	5	4	1	-	57	37
Yorks. Cup:	3	2	1	-	46	40
John Player Trophy:						
BBC2 Trophy:	1	1	-	-	13	3
Championship/ Premiership:	1	-	1	-	2	16
TOTALS:	87	49	30	8	964	739

SUMMARY OF ALL LEAGUE AND CUP GAMES
At CRAVEN PARK

	Games Played:	Hull have won	Rovers have won	Games Drawn	Points Scored Hull	Rovers
League:	52	19	31	2	563	708
R.L. Cup:	3	0	3	-	20	42
Yorks. Cup:	4	2	2	-	56	48
John Player Trophy:						
BBC2 Trophy:	2	-	2	-	16	30
Championship/ Premiership:						
TOTALS:	61	21	38	2	655	828

SUMMARY OF ALL LEAGUE AND CUP GAMES
At CRAVEN STREET

	Games Played:	Hull have won	Rovers have won	Games Drawn	Points Scored Hull	Rovers
League:	19	10	8	1	188	186
R.L. Cup:	2	2	-	-	20	5
Yorks. Cup:						
John Player Trophy:						
BBC2 Trophy:						
Championship/ Premiership:						
TOTALS:	21	12	8	1	208	193

SUMMARY OF CUP GAMES
At BOOTHFERRY PARK (The two clubs contested the John Player Trophy and Yorkshire Cup Finals here in 1984-85)

	Games Played:	Hull have won	Rovers have won	Games Drawn	Points Scored Hull	Rovers
League:						
R.L. Cup:						
Yorks. Cup:	1	1	-	-	29	12
John Player Trophy:	1	-	1	-	0	12
BBC2 Trophy:						
Championship/ Premiership:						
TOTALS:	2	1	1	-	29	24

SUMMARY OF ALL LEAGUE GAMES
At BOOTHFERRY PARK (During the period 1952-53 to 1958-59, Hull City A.F.C. loaned their ground for Rovers Home Fixture)

	Games Played:	Hull have won	Rovers have won	Games Drawn	Points Scored Hull	Rovers
League:	7	6	1	-	122	49
R.L. Cup:						
Yorks. Cup:						
John Player Trophy:						
BBC2 Trophy:						
Championship/ Premiership:						
TOTALS:	7	6	1	-	122	49

SUMMARY OF ALL CUP GAMES
At HEADINGLEY

	Games Played:	Hull have won	Rovers have won	Games Drawn	Points Scored Hull	Rovers
League:						
R.L. Cup:						
Yorks. Cup:	2	-	2	-	7	9
John Player Trophy:	1	1	-	-	12	4
BBC2 Trophy:						
Championship/ Premiership:	2	1	1	-	23	25
TOTALS:	5	2	3	-	32	38

SUMMARY OF CUP GAME
At WEMBLEY STADIUM

	Games Played:	Hull have won	Rovers have won	Games Drawn	Points Scored Hull	Rovers
League:						
R.L. Cup:	1	-	1	-	5	10
Yorks. Cup:						
John Player Trophy:						
BBC2 Trophy:						
Championship/ Premiership:						
TOTALS:	1	-	1	-	5	10

PLAYERS WHO HAVE PLAYED IN HULL v ROVERS DERBY MATCHES 1889 - 1988
(League & Cup Matches)

HULL F.C.

Player	Date of First Derby	No. of Derbys Played (Sub)	Tries	Goals	Points	Player	Date of First Derby	No. of Derbys Played (Sub)	Tries	Goals	Points
Adamson	25.12.1930	2				Bridges. K.	8.04.1983	1			
Ah Kuoi. F.	2.10.1983	10 (1)	3	1D	13	Brindle. D.	8.04.1955	1			
Allen. A.	7.10.1911	3				Britton. S.	27.10.1910	2			
Allen. A.E.	26.12.1938	5				Broadhurst. F.	7.10.1957	6			
Anderson. W.F.	12.10.1907	12				Brogden. S.	26.12.1938	2			
Appleyard. M.	9.4.1909	1				Brooks. D.	3.01.1988	1			
Arnett. C.	12.04.1985	1 (2)				Broom. E.	27.03.1964	10 (1)	1	7	17
Ashton. J.	25.12.1931	1				Brown. D.	5.10.1986	1			
Ashton. H.	31.03.1972	1				Brown. E.W.	22.03.1902	3			
Atkinson. E.	9.04.1909	1				Brown. J.	12.04.1968	4		1	2
Atkinson. H.	25.12.1925	1				Brown. R.S.	9.04.1909	1			
						Bruce. T.	12.10.1907	3		3	6
Banham. A.	26.12.1974	2	1		3	Brunyard. J.	26.12.1905	1			
Banks. B.	17.04.1981	5 (1)				Bulless. T.	20.09.1902	1			
Banks. S.J.	26.12.1906	1				Burchell. J.W.	26.12.1904	5	1		3
Barlow. G.H.	14.04.1933	14	1		3	Burnell. D.	26.12.1949	3	2		6
Barlow. L.	25.12.1934	8				Busfield. D.	31.03.1982	0 (1)			
Barnwell. K.	16.09.1961	4	1		3						
Barr. K.	24.03.1978	1				Cappleman. C.H.	26.12.1911	1			
Barrow. A.	26.11.1911	1	1		3	Carlisle. T.	19.12.1903	2			
Bateman. G.W.	25.12.1930	9	8		24	Carmichael. An.	29.03.1929	10			
Bateson. A.E.	29.09.1923	14	1	3	9	Carmichael. T.	14.12.1963	2			
Bateson. P.	7.10.1957	10		36	72	Carroll. J.	3.01.1988	1 (1)			
Batten. W.	4.10.1913	17	3		9	Carroll. W.	26.12.1904	8			
Battersby. F.	27.10.1910	1				Carvill. P.	19.12.1903	5	3		9
Baxter. L.	25.12.1950	1				Casey. L.	26.12.1972	5			
Beales. G.	26.12.1939	1				Casey. T.	27.03.1964	1			
Beardshaw. H.	25.12.1926	2	1		3	Castles. J.W.	12.10.1907	1			
Beasty. J.	26.12.1914	19				Caswell. E.	25.12.1919	24	5		15
Bedford. A.	25.12.1946	13	1		3	Clark. G.	26.02.1977	2	1		3
Blacker. B.	2.01.1989	0 (1)				Clark. J.	23.03.1951	1			
Bland. W.	16.04.1904	1				Clarkson. E.	1.10.1910	4			
Bolderson. R.W.	4.10.1924	5				Clixby. B.	16.09.1961	3			
Booth. C. (Snr)	10.04.1936	18	1		3	Coleman. C.	2.01.1989	1	1		4
Booth. C. (Jnr)	17.02.1962	4				Colling. F.	30.03.1934	3			
Booth. R.	14.12.1963	3				Collins. T.	25.12.1923	7			
Boustead. R.	21.03.1959	1	2		6	Collinson. A.	7.10.1984	1			
Bowers. A.	4.02.1939	11	3		9	Connell. G.	9.10.1909	7			
Bowman. H.	7.10.1922	24	1		3	Conway. B.	25.12.1951	7	1		3
Bowman. K.	21.09.1953	6	5		15	Cook. W.J.	20.09.1902	8	1		3
Boxall. K.	28.08.1970	16 (1)	2	19	44	Cooper. B.	8.10.1955	6			
Boyle. D.	2.01.1989	1				Cooper. C.	20.04.1973	0 (1)		1	2
Boylen. F.	26.12.1908	7	2		6	Corban. I.	17.02.1962	3			
Brand. M.	22.04.1986	2	1		4	Corner. R.	30.03.1934	9	3		9
Bray. G.	26.02.1977	9	1		3	Cornish. F.	16.09.1899	2			
Brennan. W.	29.09.1923	2				Cottrell. G.	12.10.1907	8			

Player	Date of First Derby	No. of Derbys Played (Sub)	Tries	Goals	Points
Coulman. W.	25.12.1954	2			
Coupland. P.	18.12.1979	2			
Courtney. W.J.	25.12.1929	8	1		3
Coverdale. R.	25.12.1951	9	1		3
Cowan. J.	25.12.1924	1			
Cowan. R.	31.03.1972	1			
Cowan. S.	25.12.1957	9	5		15
Cox. G.	23.03.1931	3	1		3
Crampton. J.	26.02.1977	1			
Crane. H.	25.12.1945	1			
Crane. M.	26.12.1970	17 (1)	4	1D	13
Crooks. L.	3.01.1982	13 (1)	4	13	42
Crooks. S.	5.10.1986	4			
Crowe. F.H.	15.09.1900	1	1		3
Crowther. I.D.	28.09.1980	1			
Dale. W.	16.09.1899	1			
Dannatt. A.	20.04.1984	4 (3)			
Dannatt. G.	7.10.1957	2			
Danter. T.	25.12.1948	5			
Darmody. S.	28.09.1912	6	1		3
Davidson. C.	24.03.1967	18 (3)	3	9	27
Davies. E.R.	25.12.1947	1			
Davies. R.W.	26.03.1937	1			
Davies. W.J.	3.10.1925	10			
Dawson. J.R.P.	25.12.1934	13	4		12
Day. T.	3.01.1982	4			
Dean. A.	17.04.1981	3 (1)	1	1D	4
Deane. S.	26.09.1914	1			
Dechan. J.	26.12.1908	1	2		6
Dennison. S.	18.12.1979	3	1	5	13
Devereux. J.	9.04.1909	7	2		6
Devonshire. T.	25.04.1960	20 (3)	3	1	11
Dick. K.	5.10.1986	2	1	1	6
Dickinson. W.H.	4.10.1924	1			
Dinsdale. T.	27.10.1910	1			
Divorty. G.	20.04.1984	9 (1)	1	1	6
Dockar. W.	15.04.1938	4			
Doyle-Davidson.D.	17.04.1961	12	2	1	8
Drake. J.G.	25.12.1951	13	3		9
Drake. W.D.	8.10.1955	17	3	2	13
Drew. A.	26.12.1972	0 (1)			
Driscoll. J.	16.09.1899	3			
Duke. A.	27.12.1971	10	1		3
Dunn. T.	15.09.1900	1			
Eastburn. M.	25.12.1929	1			
Eastwood. P.	6.10.1985	6	1		4
Edmonds. P.	8.04.1983	7	1		4
Edson. J.	8.04.1966	5 (1)	1		3
Eggett. C.W.	29.03.1907	1			
Elgar. N.	17.04.1987	1			
Ellerington. H.	3.04.1931	13	1		3
Ellery. C.	29.09.1923	1			
Elliott. D.	16.05.1981	1			
Ellis. J.	1.10.1921	3			
Errington. S.	25.12.1929	3			
Evans. G.	7.10.1979	3	1		3
Evans. H.	26.03.1948	2	1		3
Evans. Sam	25.04.1960	1			
Evans. Steve	31.03.1982	10	3		11
Everitt. R.G.	25.03.1932	1			
Fallon. P.	25.12.1946	2			
Farrar. V.	26.02.1978	5 (1)			
Fifield. C.R.	25.12.1931	12	2		6
Fildes. P.	16.09.1899	6			
Finn. T.	25.12.1954	20	6		18
Firth. H.	25.12.1968	10	3		9
Firth. R.	25.12.1968	2			
Fletcher. P.	3.01.1988	3			
Foreman. D.	25.12.1950	2		1	2
Forrester. J.	18.04.1919	1			
Forster. C.	12.04.1968	4 (1)			
Foulkes. K.	17.10.1964	11 (1)			
Francis. A.	1.10.1910	12	7		21
Francis. R.	25.12.1950	8	4		12
Frank. D.	16.09.1899	6	2		6
Freear. A.E.	26.12.1904	3	1		3
Fulton. H.	22.03.1902	14			
Galloway. D.	1.10.1910	1			
Gardiner. J.	26.12.1927	2			
Garrett. H.	18.04.1919	14	2		6
Garvey. R.	3.10.1925	1			
Gascoigne. A.	15.09.1985	2	1		4
Gemmell. R.	16.09.1961	10			
Geraghty. A.	28.08.1970	3 (1)			
Gerard. G.	6.10.1985	2			
Gibbons. A.	3.04.1974	1			
Gilbert. H.	28.09.1912	6	2		6
Gill. R.	25.12.1958	1			
Gittoes. K.	15.04.1949	5	1		3
Glynn. T.	25.12.1945	5	4		12
Goddard. R.T.	20.09.1902	5		5	10
Goodall. W.	26.12.1938	1			
Goodfellow. F.	26.12.1904	3		3	6
Gorman. F.	16.09.1899	4			
Gouldstone. C.	25.12.1935	1	2		6
Gwynne. T.E.	1.10.1921	15	4		12
Hall. G.	20.09.1902	6			

Player	Date of First Derby	No. of Derbys Played (Sub)	Tries	Goals	Points
Hall. P.	2.10.1977	1 (1)			
Hall. W.	26.12.1905	2			
Hall. Wilson	25.12.1928	1			
Hambling. B.	7.10.1957	7			
Hambrecht. A.	22.03.1902	1			
Hamm. B.	15.09.1900	1			
Hammill. J.	4.10.1913	4			
Hancock. B.	25.12.1967	20 (1)	4		12
Hargreaves. W.	19.12.1903	3			
Harkin. K.	3.01.1982	5			
Harmer. W.	26.12.1899	2			
Harris. P.T.	25.12.1950	24	3		9
Harrison. A.	26.12.1906	1	1		3
Harrison. C.	7.10.1979	3 (1)			
Harrison. G.	25.04.1960	1	1		3
Harrison. Jack	28.09.1912	5	4		12
Harrison. J.M.	17.01.1903	7			
Harrison. Jim	27.12.1971	2	1		3
Harrison. M.	25.12.1965	19			
Harsley.R.	25.12.1928	2			
Hart. T.	25.12.1948	9		15	30
Hattersley. S.	26.12.1939	5	1		3
Hepworth. K.	26.02.1978	3	2		6
Herberts. E.	30.03.1934	11	5	1	17
Herridge. T.	12.10.1907	19	1		3
Hewson. H.	2.10.1920	2			
Hicks. M.	3.04.1974	1			
Hicks. S.	5.10.1986	1			
Higgins. W.	28.09.1912	2			
Higo. J.	25.12.1926	1			
Hockley. N.	3.04.1953	7			
Holder. W.	12.10.1907	15			
Holdsworth. J.	18.04.1919	14	4		12
Holliday. J.A.	27.09.1919	1			
Holt. J.	25.12.1945	1			
Howlett. G.	7.10.1922	5			
Hufton. J.	21.04.1905	2			
Hughes. F.	7.10.1911	1			
Hulme. J.	18.04.1919	2			
Humphries. J.	2.10.1920	1			
Hunter. P.	2.10.1977	1			
Hurley. F.	25.12.1937	4	3		9
Hutton. C.	23.03.1951	13		28	56
Huxley. K.	17.10.1964	5 (1)			
Ibbertson. P.	27.03.1970	3	1		3
Jackson. D.	25.12.1948	4			
Jackson. L.	3.01.1988	2			
Jackson. R.W.	17.01.1903	2			
Jacques. W.	16.09.1899	4		2	4

Player	Date of First Derby	No. of Derbys Played (Sub)	Tries	Goals	Points
James. K.	7.10.1984	2			
Jefferies	25.12.1945	2			
Jenkins. E.	21.04.1905	2			
Jenney. E.	4.10.1924	12		2	4
Jervis. D.	25.12.1968	1			
Jewitt. R.	25.12.1946	3	1		3
Jimmison. S.	10.10.1946	2			
John. T.	20.09.1902	1			
Johnson. D.	25.04.1960	2	1		3
Johnson. F.	27.03.1964	1			
Johnson. T.A.	25.12.1936	9	1		3
Jones. J.M.	9.04.1909	1			
Jones. W.	15.04.1949	2			
Kavanagh. R.	25.12.1939	3			
Kear. B.	3.02.1974	1			
Keegan. A.	17.02.1962	23	1	8	19
Kemble. G.	3.01.1982	12	3		11
Kendle. M.	27.12.1971	3	1	6	15
Kennedy. J.E.	18.04.1919	18	7	28	77
Kennedy. W.	18.04.1919	2			
Kershaw. J.	25.12.1959	5	2		6
Kilburn. G.	26.12.1904	8			
Kirchin. T.	27.12.1969	9	2		6
Knapp. C.	23.03.1951	1			
Lane. S.	26.12.1974	2	1		3
Langhorn. W.	20.09.1902	5			
Larkins. C.W.	29.03.1907	2			
Lawrence. E.	25.12.1939	13	1		3
Lazenby. C.	4.04.1980	1			
Lazenby. T.	17.04.1987	0 (1)			
Lempriere. C.C.	16.09.1899	1			
Leuluai. J.	3.01.1982	15	4		14
Lewis. G.H.	19.12.1903	3			
Lewis. J.	20.09.1902	7			
Lloyd. G.	4.04.1980	3 (2)	1	10	23
Longbottom. H.	25.12.1924	3			
Low. C.A.	26.12.1899	1			
Lunn. M.	24.03.1967	1			
Lynn.T.	24.03.1978	1			
Lyon. H.	29.03.1929	5			
Macklin. A.	4.04.1969	14	4		12
Macklin. J.	14.12.1963	8		1	2
Madden. B.	26.03.1948	2	1		3
Madley. I.	17.04.1981	0 (2)			
Major. J.	26.12.1904	8			
Mallinson. W.	8.02.1986	2			
Maloney. J.	25.12.1965	16		44	88
Markham. H.	11.04.1952	11	3		9

Player	Date of First Derby	No. of Derbys Played (Sub)	Tries	Goals	Points
Markham. J.W.	2.10.1920	1			
Marshall. A.	20.04.1973	0 (1)			
Marshall. D.	26.02.1977	3		9	18
Mathers. G.E.	29.04.1933	4			
Matthews. G.	25.12.1958	10	1		3
M'Barki. H.	1.04.1988	1			
Meek. R.	26.12.1899	1			
Merry. A.J.	28.09.1912	1			
Metcalf. W.	3.04.1931	4			
Miller. F.	22.03.1902	2			
Miller. Fred.	30.03.1934	20		29	58
Mills. H.	25.12.1939	2	3		9
Mills. W.A.	18.04.1930	2	1		3
Milner. T.	26.09.1914	12	2		6
Moat. R.	8.10.1955	3	3		9
Moon. D.	2.01.1989	1	1		4
Morgan. E.	26.12.1921	11	2		6
Morgan. R.	3.09.1966	1			
Morrell. W.J.	26.12.1938	3			
Morton. A.D.	9.04.1909	4	1		3
Mountain. C.	27.03.1964	1			
Moxon. A.	19.12.1903	1			
Muggleton. J.	12.04.1985	0 (1)			4
Murray. L.	25.12.1936	1			
McCaffery. P.	3.01.1988	1			
McCoid. P.	5.10.1986	2			
McGiever. T.	4.10.1924	1			
McGlone. A.	14.12.1963	21	1	1	5
McGowan. A.	20.08.1962	3			
McNamara. E.	1.04.1967	0 (1)			
Neale. J.	27.03.1964	7			
Newlove. J.	7.10.1979	3			
Newsome. F.	27.09.1919	3			
Nicklin. B.	26.12.1949	1			
Nimb. C.	12.04.1963	1			
Noble. A.	4.04.1947	1			
Nolan. E.T.	21.04.1919	2	1		3
Norton. S.	26.02.1978	22	3		10
O'Brien. S.	25.12.1965	5	1		3
O'Hara. D.	3.01.1982	18	5		19
Oldham. J.P.	26.12.1913	6	1		3
Oliver. G.	26.12.1921	6			
Oliver. J.	25.12.1928	20	7	37	95
Oliver. N.	8.04.1966	9	4		12
Osbourne. W.T.	26.12.1906	3			
Overton. E.	25.12.1936	1			
Owbridge. M.	28.08.1970	5			
Owen. J.	12.10.1907	3	1		3
Owens. K.	16.04.1965	2	1		3
Parkes. R.A.	29.03.1907	1			
Parkinson. R.	16.09.1899	5		6	12
Parry. L.	22.03.1902	6	3		9
Patrick. S.	2.10.1983	9			
Payne. J.	15.04.1949	1			
Peacham. G.	16.05.1981	1			
Pearce. G.	3.01.1988	3	1	7+4D	22
Pearson. G.	16.04.1965	4 (1)			
Perrett. F.L.	26.12.1914	1			
Phillipson. J.	26.12.1927	5			
Pickerill. C.	7.10.1979	3			
Pickering. S.	4.10.1924	11			
Pinder. G.A.	25.12.1939	2			
Poole. B.	25.12.1948	3			
Portz. J.	12.04.1985	2			
Portz. S.	26.12.1972	3 (1)	1		3
Prendiville. P.	7.10.1979	12 (1)	3	6	21
Price. R.	1.04.1988	1 (1)			
Proctor. W.	22.09.1982	6 (4)			
Puckering. N.	20.04.1984	3 (1)			
Purcheon. G.	9.04.1909	1			
Regan. T.	3.01.1988	1			
Rhodes. R.	16.09.1899	6			
Richardson	29.04.1933	1			
Riches. W.	21.09.1953	3	1		3
Ritson. J.	22.03.1902	4	1		3
Robinson. G.	26.02.1978	4			
Robson. D.	27.12.1969	3 (1)			
Rogers. E.	26.12.1906	31	9	24	75
Rogers. G.	26.12.1908	7	1		3
Rose. P.	22.09.1982	7 (2)			
Rosenberg. W.	17.02.1962	6			
Ryan. B.	25.12.1947	5	1		3
Salmon. A.	3.02.1974	2 (2)			
Samuel. F.	25.12.1922	1			
Sanders. L.	4.04.1947	3	3		9
Saville. B.	7.10.1957	7	3		9
Schofield. E.J.	26.12.1911	1			
Schofield. G.	2.10.1983	9 (2)	4	21+1D	59
Scott. M.	26.12.1949	28	3		9
Scruton. I.	22.09.1982	1			
Shakesby. A.	10.10.1946	2			
Sharp. J.	26.12.1900	1			
Sharp. Jon.	5.10.1986	2 (1)			
Shaw. R.	26.12.1972	1	1		3
Shillito. F.W.	19.04.1946	3			
Short. M.G.	26.12.1927	5			

Player	Date of First Derby	No. of Derbys Played (Sub)	Tries	Goals	Points
Sillis. G.	16.09.1899	1			
Sinclair. A.D.	10.10.1946	7			
Skerrett. T.	17.04.1981	10			
Smailes. E.	19.04.1946	1			
Smith. J.	12.11.1960	1			
Smith. M.	16.09.1961	3			
Solal. P.	2.10.1983	1			
Sowerby. J.	29.04.1933	2			
Spamer. B.	25.12.1945	2		5	10
Spenceley. F.	15.09.1900	5			
Staples. J.	21.09.1953	1			
Stead. W.	25.03.1932	10	1		3
Stenton. I.	3.02.1974	0 (1)			
Stephenson. M.	26.02.1977	1			
Sterling. P.	27.10.1984	2			
Stevenson. G.	9.10.1909	1			
Stitt. T.	15.09.1900	3			
Stocks. G.	27.03.1964	9			
Storey. M.	1.09.1962	3			
Stone. C.	7.10.1979	11			
Stone. W.J.	27.11.1920	12	1		3
Sullivan. B.	8.05.1963	4			
Sullivan. C.	17.02.1962	18	9		27
Sullivan. J.	25.12.1946	5			
Sutton. M.	2.10.1977	2(1)			
Sutton. T.	25.04.1960	1			
Sweeting. S.	19.04.1946	1			
Sykes. C.	1.10.1956	17	1		3
Sykes. E.	27.10.1910	1			
Tanner. J.	16.09.1899	4			
Taylor. H.	2.10.1920	2			
Taylor. R.(Dick)	9.10.1909	11			
Taylor. R.(Bob)	2.10.1920	14	4		12
Taylor. W.H.	26.12.1899	18			
Teall. W.	25.03.1932	4		1	2
Thacker. L.	16.09.1933	13			
Thames	16.09.1933	1			
Thompson. F.H.	18.04.1930	7			
Thompson. J.T.	16.09.1899	7			
Tindall. J.	25.12.1945	7	4		12
Tindall. K.	20.04.1973	12 (1)			
Todd. G.	2.10.1920	3	1		3
Tomlinson. A.	22.04.1986	1	1		4
Topliss. D.	31.03.1982	6 (1)	2		7
Townend. J.	15.09.1900	2	3		9
Tripp. A.	25.12.1952	4	1		3
Trotter. N.	24.03.1967	11 (1)			
Turner. C.	15.04.1949	12	2	3	12
Turner. G.	26.02.1978	2	1	2	7

Player	Date of First Derby	No. of Derbys Played (Sub)	Tries	Goals	Points
Vass. S.	6.10.1985	1 (1)	1		4
Voyce. G.	16.09.1899	3			
Wade. J.	22.03.1902	3			
Walker. M.	26.12.1972	1			
Wallace. H.	26.12.1906	10	1	1	5
Walters. E.	25.12.1950	2			
Walters. G.	7.10.1979	3 (1)	2		6
Walters. R.	12.04.1963	2			
Walton. H.	26.12.1908	2	2		6
Wanklyn. E.	25.12.1959	1	1		3
Wardell. A.	20.04.1973	4 (1)			
Watkinson. J.	3.04.1953	2			
Watt. G.	25.12.1947	6			
Watts. I.	25.12.1945	20	15		45
Welham. P.	3.01.1988	2 (1)	1		4
Whitehead. T.	20.08.1962	2			
Whiteley. J.	25.12.1950	24	8		24
Whiteley. P.	21.03.1959	4			
Whitty. S.	25.12.1922	12	1		3
Wilby. T.	4.04.1980	6	1		3
Wileman. R.	7.10.1979	8	1		3
Wiles. H.	16.09.1899	4			
Wilkinson. C.	14.04.1933	4			
Wilkinson. H.	25.12.1939	3			
Williams. G.	26.12.1972	1			
Wilson. I.	28.08.1980	1			
Wilson. S.	10.04.1936	7	3		9
Windley. P.	22.04.1986	1			
Winsor. F.	18.04.1930	6	1		3
Wood. F.	19.12.1903	1			
Wood. F.	3.04.1931	2			
Woodhead. H.	15.09.1900	3			
Woods. P.	18.12.1979	4		7	14
Wray. E.	15.04.1938	3			
Wray. G.E.	18.04.1930	1			
Wyburn. J.E.	26.09.1914	13	1		3
Young. P.	24.03.1978	1			

HULL KINGSTON ROVERS

Player	Date of First Derby	No. of Derbys Played (Sub)	Tries	Goals	Points
Ackerley. A.	21.03.1959	4			
Agar. A.	26.02.1977	3 (1)	1		3
Allen. W.	21.04.1919	1			
Anderson. M.	11.04.1952	5			
Armitage. P.	25.12.1951	2		1	2
Atkinson. S.	25.12.1945	6	2		6
Austin. G.	18.04.1919	24	7	2	25
Austin. P.	25.12.1953	2			
Ballantyne. G.	18.09.1967	1			
Bangs. P.	7.10.1957	1			
Barker. G.	25.12.1947	5			
Barlow. R.H.	26.12.1908	1			
Barnard. E.	26.12.1972	1			
Barraclough. J.	25.12.1946	9			
Barron. F.	26.12.1908	4	3		9
Barry. J.	22.03.1902	10	1		3
Bartliffe. A.	8.10.1955	1			
Bateman. G.W.	25.12.1925	8	1		3
Bateman. T.	27.09.1919	1			
Bath. J.	17.10.1964	1			
Batten. W. (Jnr)	3.04.1931	6	3		9
Beall. M.	22.04.1986	4 (1)			
Beaumont. H.	30.03.1934	7		2	4
Beaumont. L.	25.12.1934	10	2		6
Beaumont. W.	25.12.1945	5	1		3
Beck. B.	21.09.1953	4	1	1	5
Bedford. E.	25.12.1939	4			
Beetson. A.	25.12.1968	1			
Bent. W.	26.12.1906	2			
Bielby. F.	18.04.1919	20	3		9
Biggs. W.	26.12.1907	2			
Binks. H.	25.12.1923	17	1		3
Bishop. D.	2.01.1989	1			
Blackmore. J.	1.10.1910	4			
Blackmore. M.	1.09.1962	9	5		15
Blanchard. L.	26.12.1938	5			
Blossom. F.	25.03.1932	4			
Boagey. F.	26.12.1921	13	1		3
Boagey. R.	25.12.1919	5			
Boltman. P.	26.12.1911	1			
Bonner. E.	16.09.1961	5	1		3
Booth. A.	12.10.1907	4			
Bourton. T.	30.03.1956	2			
Boustead. K.	5.10.1986	2	1		4
Bradshaw. W.	26.09.1914	8	2	6	18
Boylen. F.	18.04.1919	4			
Brain. C.	26.12.1908	10	2	1	8
Bratley. H.	25.12.1945	1			
Briggs. D.	25.12.1952	1			
Brindle. F.	25.12.1930	6			
Britton. B.	4.10.1924	14	1		3
Broadhurst. M.	2.10.1983	7			
Brook. B.	12.04.1968	3			
Brookfield. L.	30.03.1956	3			
Brown. C.	30.03.1934	1			
Brown. J.	9.04.1971	3			
Brown. T.H.	26.12.1914	1			
Buckle. T.	21.09.1953	8		8	16
Bullock. H.	25.12.1919	1			
Bunting. A.	25.12.1959	14 (1)	3		9
Burton. C.	17.04.1981	11 (3)	1		3
Burwell. A.	25.12.1959	10	7		21
Burwell. B.	16.09.1961	4			
Carde. J.	17.01.1903	1			
Cardy. R.	31.03.1972	1			
Carmichael. A.	16.04.1904	20		35	70
Carmichael. A.	25.12.1924	3			
Carmichael. G.	18.04.1930	11	3	13	35
Casey. L.	26.02.1977	11			
Cavill. R.W.	26.12.1907	2			
Cayzer. J.	12.09.1936	7	1		3
Chalkley. D.	3.04.1953	1		1	2
Chamberlain. L.	12.04.1963	1			
Chambers. O.	26.12.1906	1			
Chapman. J.	15.04.1949	1			
Clark. G.	22.09.1982	12	6		24
Clark. L.	1.05.1963	4	1	3	9
Clark. P.	26.12.1949	2			
Clark. W.	18.04.1919	12	1		3
Clarke. L.	25.12.1934	9			
Clarke. L.	7.04.1950	1			
Clarkson. G.	7.10.1979	2			
Clawson. T.	25.12.1968	7		17	34
Close. C.	2.01.1989	1	1		4
Cole. J.	15.09.1900	3			
Cook. J.	25.12.1919	24	3		9
Cooper. B.	25.12.1967	1			
Cooper. C.	16.04.1965	11			
Cooper. D.	2.10.1920	1			
Cornforth. W.	25.12.1950	2	1		3
Coulman. W.	25.12.1959	2			
Coulson. B.	1.10.1956	9	1		3
Coulson. G.	25.12.1956	2			
Coupland. P.	25.12.1967	13 (1)	2	4	14

Player	Date of First Derby	No. of Derbys Played (Sub)	Tries	Goals	Points
Coverdale. R.	4.04.1958	10			
Crane. M.	4.04.1980	1	1		3
Craven. B.	26.10.1910	3	1		3
Croft. B.	30.03.1956	3			
Crooks. S.	7.10.1979	5 (2)	1		3
Crosby. A.	26.12.1970	1			
Cunningham. J.	2.10.1977	2	1		3
Daddy. M.	25.12.1939	8	1		3
Dakin. R.W.	27.12.1909	1			
Dale. H.	25.12.1928	13	3		9
Daley. P.	26.12.1970	3 (1)			
Danter. T.	25.12.1956	1			
Dawson. N.	27.12.1971	4 (1)		2	4
Dean. I.L.	28.09.1912	6		2	4
Debney. J.	16.09.1899	4			
Deeley. G.	30.03.1934	1			
Dilcock. W.H.	29.03.1907	6	4		12
Dixon. C.	28.09.1980	1			
Dockar. A.	25.12.1939	17	3	9	27
Dorahy. J.	20.04.1984	5	2	16	40
Douglas. G.	28.09.1980	0 (1)			
Downing. K.	26.12.1970	1			
Drake. Jim.	17.02.1962	5			
Drake. Joe.	25.04.1960	1			
Dunn. G.	3.02.1972	11	3		9
Eastwood. J.	30.03.1934	13	5		15
Eddoms. W.	14.04.1933	8			
Edmonds. J.	14.04.1934	2			
Edmonds. P.	31.03.1982	0 (1)			
Egan. W.	11.04.1952	1			
Elliott. D.	25.12.1958	17 (2)	3		9
Ellis. G.	26.12.1900	10			
Ema. A.	7.10.1984	10 (1)			
Evans. R.	7.10.1957	2			
Evans. Sam.	21.09.1953	4		5	10
Fairbairn. G.	3.01.1982	16	2	25+3D	60
Farnhill. K.	25.12.1959	1			
Farr. S.	22.04.1986	1			
Feetham. J.	25.12.1926	6	2		6
Feetham. W.	20.09.1902	1			
Fenton. J.	29.03.1907	1			
Ferguson. A.	26.12.1949	1	1		3
Fishwick. G.	4.04.1958	1		1	2
Fitzgibbon. A.	3.02.1974	1			
Flanagan. P.	12.11.1960	30	5	1D	16
Flannery. S.	24.03.1967	1	1		3
Fletcher. G.	16.09.1899	7	1		3
Fletcher. M.	22.04.1986	3		7	14

Player	Date of First Derby	No. of Derbys Played (Sub)	Tries	Goals	Points
Forth. W.G.	25.12.1951	1			
Foster. F.	16.05.1965	9		1	2
Foster. J.W.	22.03.1902	1			
Foster. L.	12.04.1968	2			
Fox. F.	14.12.1963	7			
Fox. N.	26.12.1974	1	1	5	13
Fox. P.	1.05.1963	1			
Freeman. J.	26.12.1900	1			
Fridlington. R.	14.04.1933	2			
Fussey. L.	31.10.1914	5			
Garry. A.	21.09.1953	8			
Garton. G.	7.10.1957	2			
Gath. J.	20.09.1902	8			
Gay. R.	27.12.1969	0 (1)			
Gee. H.	25.12.1945	2	1		3
Gibson. F.	18.04.1919	10		5	10
Gillie. C.L.	4.10.1913	1			
Gilmore. J.	26.12.1914	1			
Golder. B.	8.04.1955	2			
Goldswain. B.	25.12.1945	8			
Gordon. J.	17.01.1903	8		2	4
Gorman. F.	19.12.1903	3			
Goulding. K.	8.04.1955	2	1		3
Goulding. R.	17.01.1903	2			
Grice. K.	25.12.1954	9	1		3
Griffett. H.	4.04.1958	1			
Guy. W.	16.09.1899	7	1		3
Hackling. G.	25.04.1960	1			
Hall. D.	3.02.1974	19 (1)	4	2	16
Hall. J.	26.12.1927	1			
Hall. Jim A.	25.12.1968	0 (1)			
Hall. John.	8.10.1955	3	1		3
Hambrecht. C.J.	26.12.1906	5			
Hancock. N.	30.03.1956	3			
Harbour. K.	25.12.1953	3			
Harkin. P.	4.04.1980	9 (2)		1D	1
Harper. C.	25.12.1956	1			
Harris. L.	27.11.1920	18	4		12
Harris. R.	25.02.1961	8	3		9
Harrison. A.	25.12.1937	1			
Harrison. C.	22.04.1986	1			
Harrison. Dave.	1.04.1988	2	1		4
Harrison. Des.	15.09.1985	6 (1)			
Hartley. L.	10.10.1946	2			
Hartley. S.	27.12.1971	19 (4)	6		18
Hatch. B.	20.08.1962	2			
Henson. E.W.	26.12.1899	1			
Heslop. D.	31.03.1972	6			
Hick. D.	26.12.1972	2			

Player	Date of First Derby	No. of Derbys Played (Sub)	Tries	Goals	Points
Hicks. R.G.	28.09.1912	4			
Hickson. J.	18.09.1967	5 (3)			
Hill. R.	25.12.1930	5			
Hill. V.	25.12.1945	4			
Hogan. P.	7.10.1979	17 (1)	7	2	28
Hodgson. E.	26.12.1913	1	1		3
Holdstock. A.	16.09.1961	1			
Holdstock. R.	20.04.1973	11 (2)	1		4
Holland. D.	4.04.1958	4			
Holliday. W.	16.04.1965	10		13	26
Holt. J.	25.12.1953	1			
Horner. W.	26.12.1913	1			
Hotham. J.	29.03.1907	2			
Hoult. J.	7.10.1922	11	6		18
Hubbard. S.	7.10.1979	11	6	17	52
Hudson. T.	27.12.1971	5		1	2
Hughes. M.	26.02.1977	2			
Hughes. R.	9.04.1909	9	1	1	5
Huskins. W.	9.10.1909	12	1		3
Hutchinson. B.	15.04.1938	1	1		3
Hutchinson. C.	22.04.1986	1			
Hyam. W.	1.10.1910	4	2		6
Ingram. P.	25.12.1950	2			
Irvine. J.	2.01.1989	1			
Jackson. A.	30.03.1934	1			
Jackson. R.W.	16.09.1899	1			
Jackson. W.	25.12.1947	2	1		3
Jacques. K.	25.12.1958	4			
Jenkin. J.	21.03.1959	4			
Johnson. D.	1.10.1956	1			
Johnson. L.	22.04.1986	1			
Johnson. R.	15.09.1900	2			
Jones. R.	26.12.1910	1			
Jones. W.	18.04.1930	1			
Jordan. A.J.	25.12.1928	4			
Jowett. W.F.	26.12.1906	2			
Keegan. J.	27.03.1959	1			
Keegan. R.	25.12.1919	1			
Kellett. C.	7.10.1957	22		64	128
Kelly. A.	8.04.1983	6 (2)	3		12
Kemp. A.	16.09.1899	10	1	1	5
Key. P.	30.03.1956	8	1		3
Kingsbury. K.	25.04.1960	2		2	4
Kirk. G.	20.09.1902	1			
Kirk. M.	12.11.1960	1			
Kirkpatrick. G.	3.02.1972	3	1		3
Kitson. H.	25.12.1919	1			
Knapp. E.	21.09.1953	1			
Knowelden. B.	11.04.1952	4			
Kruger. H.	15.09.1900	1			
Last. C.	25.04.1960	1			
Laws. D.	8.04.1983	12	2		8
Lazenby. T.	8.04.1983	1 (1)			
Leighton. S.	3.02.1974	2			
Levett. J.	16.09.1899	2			
Lewis. A.	16.09.1933	2	1		3
Lewis. C.	22.03.1902	1			
Lewis. D.	28.09.1912	2	1		3
Lewis. H.	11.04.1952	1			
Lewis. J.	26.12.1949	3		6	12
Lockwood. A.	1.05.1963	1			
Lockwood. B.	26.02.1978	5			
Lofthouse. A.	26.12.1906	3			
Longstaff. P.	25.12.1967	8	1		3
Lord. H.	4.10.1913	5			
Lowe. J.	26.09.1914	3			
Lowe. P.	18.09.1967	26 (2)	5		15
Lydiat. J.	8.04.1983	6 (4)		5	10
Lyons. S.	26.12.1974	2			
Madley. I.	1.01.1975	1			
Madley. W.	22.03.1902	7	1	2	7
Mageen. J.	4.04.1958	1	1		3
Major. T.	25.04.1960	18	3		9
Mann. A.	9.10.1909	14	1		3
Markham. I.	4.04.1969	9	1		3
Marrow. F.	16.04.1904	1			
Maskill. R.	12.09.1936	8			
Matthews. A.	7.10.1957	1			
Matthews. B.	25.02.1961	3			
Megson. G.	10.10.1946	1			
Mennell. B.	25.12.1965	5			
Middleton. F.	26.03.1937	2			
Miller. B.	12.04.1985	0 (1)			
Miller. G.	26.01.1985	6	2		8
Millington. J.	27.12.1971	15 (4)	1		3
Mills. H.	25.12.1946	8			
Mills. R.	19.04.1946	10	2	8	22
Millward. R.	3.09.1966	19	3	15+2D	41
Milner. J.C.	4.02.1939	2			
Moat. R.	25.12.1958	4			
Moore. A.	9.04.1909	24	6		18
Moore. F.	25.12.1950	6	1		3
Moore. J.	3.04.1953	1			
Moore. John.	27.03.1963	22 (1)	8		24
Moores. J.H.	14.04.1933	3			
Morfitt. S.	26.12.1899	3			
Morgan. S.	25.12.1937	6	1		3

Player	Date of First Derby	No. of Derbys Played (Sub)	Tries	Goals	Points
Mortimer. P.	3.01.1988	1			
Moss. A.	19.04.1935	1			
Moxon. R.	26.12.1938	2	1		3
Mullineux. D.	26.12.1904	4	1		3
Mullins. A.	12.11.1960	6			
Mulvey. H.	2.10.1920	4	1		3
Murphy. P.	20.08.1962	1	1		3
Muscroft. P.	17.04.1981	5			
McAvoy. J.	25.12.1951	4	2		6
McBain. F.	25.12.1946	4	3		9
McConnell. W.	22.03.1902	1			
McDonald. C.	26.12.1910	4	1		3
McGiever. T.	26.12.1913	12	1		3
McGlone. J.	26.12.1921	1			
Mc.Gowan. T.	19.04.1935	3			
McHugh. G.	28.09.1980	0 (1)			
McIntyre. J.	7.10.1922	20	2		6
McNamara. E.	14.12.1963	1			
McNulty. J.	25.12.1937	1			
McWatt. W.	19.04.1935	21		20	40
Naylor. J.	7.04.1939	1			
Neale. J.	3.02.1972	3			
Ness. W.	25.12.1945	2			
Nicholls. J.	19.04.1946	1	1		3
Noble. J.	16.09.1899	1			
Noble. R.	22.04.1986	1			
Oates. L.	15.04.1949	2			
O'Connor. H.	25.12.1950	1			
O'Leary. P.	25.12.1954	2			
Oliver. F.W.	26.12.1913	3			
Oliver. J.	15.04.1938	3		2	4
Olsen. S.	22.04.1986	1			
Osborne. L.	27.11.1920	25		33	66
Osbourne. W.T.	26.12.1904	3			
Palframan. A.	26.03.1948	10			
Palmer. E.	27.03.1963	3 (2)			
Parker. F.	22.04.1986	0 (1)			
Parker. J.	25.12.1954	4		1	2
Parker. W.	22.04.1986	5	3	2D	14
Parkin. J.	25.12.1930	4	1		3
Paul. G.	21.03.1959	14	8		24
Payne. A.	26.12.1949	2			
Peak.	18.04.1919	2			
Perrott. W.	25.12.1936	2			
Phillips. J.	12.09.1936	1			
Phipps. W.	26.12.1900	11	2		6
Pickering. J.	17.01.1903	2			

Player	Date of First Derby	No. of Derbys Played (Sub)	Tries	Goals	Points
Pollard. K.	25.12.1965	0 (1)			
Poole. H.	25.02.1961	9	1		3
Porter. M.	2.01.1989	1			
Pratt. G.	26.12.1906	5	2		6
Pratt. R.	2.01.1989	1			
Prescott. J.H.	26.09.1914	4			
Price. R.	28.09.1980	2			
Proctor. P.	17.04.1981	2 (1)			
Prohm. G.	22.09.1982	11	3		12
Rainton. C.	25.12.1930	2			
Ramsden. J.	25.12.1934	23	2		6
Raynor. J.	3.10.1925	1			
Read. J.W.	17.01.1903	6	1		3
Read. S.	29.03.1907	1	1		3
Rees. D.	13.04.1906	3			
Rees. R.	11.03.1922	7	1		3
Rhoades. R.W.	3.10.1925	2	1		3
Rhodes. J.	16.09.1899	5			
Riach. F.	19.04.1935	1			
Richards. E.	10.10.1946	6	5		15
Richardson. T.E.	26.12.1907	2			
Riley. W.	4.04.1958	7			
Ripton. T.	16.09.1899	1			
Roberts. F.	6.04.1928	3			
Robinson. A.W.	26.12.1899	5		1	2
Robinson. I.	2.10.1977	10	2	1	10
Rogers. J.	25.12.1958	2			
Rooms. M.	28.08.1970	3 (1)	1		3
Rose. P.	28.08.1970	11 (2)	2		6
Rowbottom. R.	25.12.1959	1			
Rudd. C.	20.04.1984	2 (2)			
Ruddeforth. S.	16.09.1899	1			
Rushton. D.	25.12.1951	5	1		3
Ryan. G.	3.01.1988	2			
Saddington. G.E.	6.04.1928	11			
Sanderson. J.	17.04.1981	1			
Sandham. W.	9.04.1909	11	3		9
Saul. G.	15.04.1927	2			
Scarborough. A.	6.04.1928	2			
Schofield. J.	26.03.1948	2			
Scholes. D.	15.04.1949	6	2		6
Sedgwick. J.	26.12.1908	1			
Senior. A.	25.12.1946	3			
Sharpe. L.	25.12.1928	9	1		3
Shaw. B.	30.03.1956	5	1		3
Sherwood. H.	26.12.1906	3			
Sherwood. S.	26.12.1906	2			
Shiel. W.	4.10.1913	1			
Shillito. F.	25.12.1934	6	1		3

Player	Date of First Derby	No. of Derbys Played (Sub)	Tries	Goals	Points
Shipp. T.H.	25.12.1934	1			
Shires. J.	8.04.1955	3	1		3
Sims. G.	22.04.1986	1			
Sims. W.	22.03.1902	1			
Sinclair. H.	16.09.1899	8		1	2
Sissons. A.	22.04.1986	1			
Small. P.	4.04.1969	2			
Smith. C.	25.12.1947	3			
Smith. D.	30.03.1956	1	1		3
Smith. G.	8.04.1983	11 (1)	2	1D	9
Smith. H.W.	26.12.1906	1			
Smith. J.	14.04.1933	1			
Smith. M.	26.02.1977	25 (1)	11	1D	40
Smith. Sam.	25.12.1950	6			
Smith. Steve.	22.04.1986	2			
Smithies. R.	26.12.1972	3	2		6
Spackman. A.	26.12.1904	12	1		3
Spamer. J.	15.04.1927	25	7		21
Speckman. P.	22.04.1986	2			
Speckman. R.	25.12.1959	1			
Spence. B.	25.12.1950	2			
Spivey. G.	7.10.1911	2	2		6
Starks. A.	16.09.1899	13	2	3	12
Stead. R.	22.04.1986	3 (1)			
Steele. C.	25.12.1947	3			
Stephenson. J.	16.09.1899	5			
Stephenson. M.	25.12.1965	13 (1)	4		12
Stocks. T.	16.09.1961	1	2		6
Sullivan. C.	26.12.1974	10	3		9
Surman. T.	1.10.1910	2	1		3
Sutton. T.	25.12.1951	8			
Sykes. C.	9.04.1971	1			
Sykes. R.	27.12.1909	4			
Tate. G.	7.04.1950	2	1		3
Tattersfield. E.	29.04.1933	9	1	1	5
Taylor. J.	22.03.1902	1			
Taylor. John.	25.12.1958	10	2		6
Taylor. R.	3.01.1988	1			
Taylor. T.	26.12.1907	2			
Teall. W.	26.12.1939	1		2	4
Thomas. P.	9.04.1909	6	2		6
Thompson. Alb.	17.04.1961	2			
Thompson. Andy.	17.04.1987	1			
Thompson. F.	19.04.1935	5			
Thornton. M.	25.12.1953	3			
Tong. J.	25.12.1951	9			
Tonks. L.	26.12.1970	1			
Townsley. R.	20.09.1902	6			
Trowell. C.	25.02.1961	1			
Trump. L.C.	28.09.1912	7			

Player	Date of First Derby	No. of Derbys Played (Sub)	Tries	Goals	Points
Tullock. G.	26.12.1949	11	2		6
Tullock. H.	16.09.1899	3	1	4	11
Turner. D.	25.12.1951	6	1		3
Tyreman. G.	18.12.1979	1			
Tyrer. C.	26.02.1977	3		8	16
Unsworth. G.	26.12.1908	2			
Van Rooyen. G.	7.10.1922	3			
Vaughan. D.	26.09.1914	3	3		9
Wainwright. D.	1.04.1967	7 (1)			
Wallis. C.	25.12.1968	9	1		3
Walsh. J.	31.03.1982	2			
Walshaw. H.	30.03.1934	2	1		3
Walters. R.	7.10.1957	1			
Ward. T.	26.12.1899	3			
Warters. G.	25.12.1951	1			
Watkinson. D.	26.02.1978	20		1D	1
Watson. A.	26.12.1911	5			
Watson. B.	26.12.1974	9	1		3
Watson. K.	31.03.1982	1			
Webb. C.A.	4.10.1924	2			
Welsby. H.	25.12.1948	2			
West. G.H.	22.03.1902	12	2	1	8
Westerdale. C.W.	2.10.1920	23	2		6
Westerdale. F.	25.12.1930	1			
White. G.	25.12.1935	4			
White. P.	9.04.1909	1			
Whitton. G.	25.12.1935	4			
Wiley. S.	27.12.1969	4			
Wilkinson. J.H.	27.11.1920	15	2		6
Wilkinson. J.R.	2.10.1920	19			
Willett. R.	28.08.1970	2	1		3
Williams. C.	15.09.1900	1			
Williams. H.	25.12.1929	7	1		3
Wilmot. P.	19.04.1946	5			
Wilson. E.	25.12.1958	1			
Windle. A.	16.09.1899	15			
Windmill. D.	26.12.1972	2	1		3
Winsor. F.	19.04.1935	2			
Wood. A.	16.09.1933	4	2		6
Woodcock. J.	16.09.1933	2			
Wootton. W.T.	26.09.1914	6	1	4	11
Wrigglesworth. G.	25.12.1965	4			
Young. Chris.	25.12.1965	11	3		9
Young. George.	25.12.1950	3			
Young. Gordon.	25.12.1965	7 (1)			
Young. V.	12.09.1936	2	2		6
Youngman. W.	28.09.1980	1	2		6

DUAL ROLES

A total of 75 players have turned out for both clubs, while John Whiteley played for Hull and then coached Rovers as did Colin Hutton and W. Jacques. Arthur Bunting played for Rovers and coached Hull. The list in alphabetical order is:-

S. Atkinson (WG)	T. Danter	J. Neale
G.W. Bateman	J. Eastwood (WG)	W. Ness (WG)
H. Beaumont (WG)	J. Edmonds (WG)	E.T. Nolan
L. Beaumont (WG)	P. Edmonds	P. O'Leary
A. Bedford	Sam Evans	F.W. Oliver
L. Bedford	P. Flanagan	J. Oliver
L. Blanchard (WG)	L. Foster	W.T. Osbourne
F. Boylen	N. Gillard	J. Ramsden (WG)
E.W. Brown	F. Gorman	P. Rose
Joe Brown	A. Holdstock	L. Sanders
Andrew Carmichael	J. Holt	L. Sharpe (WG)
L. Casey	P. Ingram	F.W. Shillito
L. Clark (WG)	R.W. Jackson	B. Spamer
T. Clawson	A. Kilby	J. Stephenson
A. Codd (WG)	T. Kirchin	M. Stephenson
C. Cooper	John Lamping	C. Sullivan
W. Coulman	T. Lazenby	T. Sutton
P. Coupland	T. Lynn	C. Sykes
R. Coverdale	I. Madley	E. Tattersfield
B. Coverley	T. McGiever	— Tidy
M. Crane	E. McNamara	G. Turner
S. Crooks	W. McWatt (WG)	R. Walters
M. Daddy	H. Mills	G. White
A. Dockar	R. Mills	F. Winsor
Jim Drake	R. Moat	W. Teal (WG)

WG=War Guest. Rovers provided guest players for Hull during both World Wars when Hull continued playing.

INDIVIDUAL RECORDS IN DERBY MATCHES

Most Appearances

HULL		ROVERS	
E. Rogers	31	P. Flanagan	30
M. Scott	28	P. Lowe	26+ 2 Sub
H. Bowman	24	M. Smith	25+ 1 Sub
E. Caswell	24	L. Osborne	25
P.T. Harris	24	J. Spamer	25
J. Whiteley	24	G. Austin	24
A. Keegan	23	J. Cook	24
S. Norton	22	A. Moore	24

Note: Clive Sullivan played 18 Derby's for Hull and a further 10 for Rovers making a total of 28.

Most Tries

HULL		ROVERS	
I. Watts	15	Mike Smith	11
E. Rogers	9	John Moore	8
C. Sullivan	9*	G. Paul	8
G.W. Bateman	8	G. Austin	7
J. Whiteley	8	A. Burwell	7
		P. Hogan	7

* Clive Sullivan also scored 3 Tries for Rovers in Derby matches making a total of 12.

Most Goals

HULL		ROVERS	
J. Maloney	44	C. Kellett	64
J. Oliver	37	A. Carmichael	35
P. Bateson	36	L. Osborne	33
F. Miller	29	G. Fairburn	28

Most Points

HULL		ROVERS	
J. Oliver	95	C. Kellett	128
J. Maloney	88	A. Carmichael	70
J. Kennedy	77	L. Osborne	66
E. Rogers	75	G. Fairbairn	60
P. Bateson	72	S. Hubbard	52
C. Hutton	56		

SCORING ACHIEVEMENTS IN A MATCH

Tries

HULL		ROVERS	
4	T. Glynn . . . . (25.Dec.1945)	3	J. Hoult . . . . (4.Oct.1924)
4	I. Watts . . . . . (25.Dec.1953)	3	A. Burwell . . . . . (4.Apr.1969)
4	I. Watts . . . . . (25.Dec.1956)		
3	J. Townend . (26.Dec.1900)		
3	E. Rogers . . . (26.Dec.1908)		
3	T.E. Gwynne (25.Dec.1923)		
3	F. Hurley . . . . (25.Dec.1937)		
3	H. Mills . . . . . (26.Dec.1939)		
3	L. Sanders . . . . (7.Apr.1950)		
3	K. Bowman. . . (30.Mar.1956)		
3	C. Sullivan . . (28.Aug.1970)		

Goals

HULL		ROVERS	
8	G. Schofield (20.Apr.1984)	7	C. Kellett . . (17.Oct.1964)
7	J. Maloney . (9.Apr.1971)	7	S. Hubbard . (4.Apr.1980)
		7	R. Millward . (4.Apr.1969)

(No other player has scored more than 6 goals in a game)

Points

HULL		ROVERS	
16	G. Schofield . (20.Apr.1984)	16	J. Dorahy . . . . (5.Oct.1986)
15	J. Oliver. . . . (16.Sept.1933)		

Consecutive Appearances in Derby Matches

G. Austin (Rovers) appeared in 24 consecutive matches; in fact this was his sum total of Derby appearances.

M. Scott clocked up 23 consecutive Derby appearances for Hull.

J. Oliver completed 20 consecutive Derby appearances for Hull and then played in the next 3 for Rovers following his transfer in 1938.

Consecutive Victories in Derby Combat

It is a testimony to the great sense of competition and rivalry between the two clubs, that there have rarely been long periods where the results were dominated by one side or the other. There have been only 3 instances of one or other side scoring more than 5 consecutive victories. Hull registered 10 wins in the period 16 Sept. 1933 to 25 Dec. 1937 and then set the record with 12 straight victories from 30. March 1956 to 25. Feb. 1961. Curiously, Rovers' record of 10 successive victories then followed straight on from 17. April 1961 to 17. Oct. 1964.

FINAL MEMORIES

All of the 'Derby' meetings during the past 90 years will have created their own memories for those that witnessed them. It would seem certain, however, that the nine Cup Finals contested by the pair will be remembered and talked of more readily.

Billy Bradshaw's dropped goal in the 1920 Yorkshire Cup Final giving Rovers victory at a time when thousands were already on the trams going back to Leeds Station convinced that a replay was to be faced; Gibson's missed conversion in the final moments of the 1921 Championship Final leaving Hull Champions for a second year, and Alan Burwell's late try against a badly-limping 'Nobby' Oliver in the Yorkshire Cup final of 1967. All dramatic, late, incidents which meant Joy or Despair to each and every spectator.

The next three Finals, in contrast, were virtually settled quite early in the proceedings. Steve Dennison's early try and conversion represented a winning score in the 1979-80 BBC2 Final; Steve Hubbard's ranging try from an astute Brian Lockwood pass, together with the penalty goal, awarded for a foul on him as he scored, similarly sealed Hull's fate at Wembley later the same season; long range tries from Steve Hartley and Phil Hogan before halftime left Hull with too big a mountain to climb in the 1981 Premiership encounter, at Headingley.

One try certain to be talked of for many a year was the effort by Ronnie Wileman in the 1982 John Player Trophy Final at Headingley. Muscroft had left his wing unguarded as Wileman was acting half-back on the halfway line. He scuttled off down the best stand side and, alas, George Fairbairn had been left with acres to have to cover. Wileman won the race to the corner and Hull were as good as home.

Rovers were to exact revenge in the same competition three years later at Boothferry Park. But not before Hull had at last taken a Yorkshire Cup Final at their rivals' expense. Coming into the Final as winners of the Trophy for the previous two seasons, it looked as though Hull's tenure was about to come to grief as Rovers burst through for three tries by the half-hour mark. Rovers then fell victim to the brilliance of Australian scrum-half, Peter Sterling, and the craft of 2nd Row, Steve Norton. Sterling put a short kick across to the posts for Lee Crooks to score. The conversion and a penalty from Gary Schofield put Hull back in the game with a halftime score of 8-12. Two minutes after the break, full back Gary Kemble fielded a Rovers drop - out on the halfway line and broke clean through to score on the right. Hull never looked back and added further tries by Kemble, Norton and Evans. Thus, Hull had performed the 'Hat Trick' of Yorkshire Cup Wins, and had performed a 'Houdini' act in so doing.

Yes, there is a memory for every witness to a Derby encounter. These Finals cover but nine of the whole series of matches. But they each represented, in their individual way, all that is best in Rugby League. They all engender the spirit — 'Love thy neighbour by all means — after you've beaten him!'